Pentecostals and the Poor

Reflections from the Indian Context

Ivan M. Satyavrata

Foreword by Byron D. Klaus

WIPF & STOCK · Eugene, Oregon

Wipf and Stock Publishers
199 W 8th Ave, Suite 3
Eugene, OR 97401

Pentecostals and the Poor
Reflections from the Indian Context
By Satyavrata, Ivan M. and Klaus, Byron D.
Copyright©2017 APTS Press
ISBN 13: 978-1-5326-3395-9
Publication date 5/31/2017
Previously published by APTS Press, 2017

This edition is published by Wipf and Stock Publishers under license from APTS Press.

Publisher's Preface
to the Occasional Papers Series

With this publication, we are pleased to announce the beginning of a new series of books entitled *The APTS Press Occasional Papers Series*.

The purpose of this series to produce smaller books comprised of articles that deal with theological, anthropological and missiological issues relevant to serving God in Asia. From time to time, other sciences may also be so employed. As the title suggests, the books will be published as articles of interest to our readers become available.

For further information on this series or other work of the APTS Press, including our journal, the *Asian Journal of Pentecostal Studies*, please visit our website, www.apts.edu, and send an email to the attention of the director of APTS Press.

Sincerely,

Teresa Chai, PhD.
Dave Johnson, Dmiss.
Series Editors

Author's Preface

The immediate occasion for my reflection on this theme was an invitation from the Asia Pacific Theological Association [APTA] to address their General Assembly at Chiang Mai, Thailand, in the Fall of 2011. I was asked to present four lectures, reflecting on the topic of *Power, Tradition & Social Engagement*, with a focus on how these themes may be integrated in theological education and the equipping of leaders for ministry in Asia.

Although the theme was not my selection, it was not long before I found myself deeply absorbed in it for several reasons. To begin with, my personal spiritual journey had involved exposure to several older Christian traditions. My paternal grandfather was a Presbyterian minister in the German Basel Mission, which had a strong presence along the south west coast of India during the earlier years of Protestant missions in India. My parents, however, attended a Methodist Church during my growing years in the city of Bombay (now Mumbai) and later became members of an Evangelical Alliance Church. My schooling was in a Church of England school, but it was the Charismatic movement in Bombay that shaped my discipleship following my conversion at the age of seventeen. Later, I found my church home in the Assemblies of God.

My subsequent theological journey exposed me to influences from a wide variety of traditions, including Pentecostal, Brethren, Baptist, Reformed Anglican and Roman Catholic. Whenever I heard references being made to the "Reformed" tradition or "Anglican" tradition or "Roman Catholic" tradition, I would often wonder whether it would be appropriate to speak of a "Pentecostal" tradition and, if so, how should it be described? My research led me to conclude that not only was it appropriate to refer to a Pentecostal tradition, but that despite some challenges of characterization posed by the diverse nature of the Pentecostal movement, the "traditioning" process was in fact an urgent necessity. Failure to do so in a timely manner could result in the emergence of inauthentic and inadequate depictions of the Pentecostal tradition that fail to fairly represent its roots and distinctives. These papers are a small contribution towards a broader ongoing global task that I trust more Pentecostal scholars will pay attention to in future.

A second reason this theme gripped my interest was because it brought together two of my deepest passions in ministry. My earliest years in ministry were spent as a grass-roots evangelist in the streets and slums of Bombay. I was engaged subsequently in church-planting efforts, first in downtown Bombay and then in a city in North India. When I joined the faculty at Southern Asia Bible College (now Centre for Global Leadership Development), Bangalore, it was because of the promise it held for raising leaders who would powerfully impact Christ's Church-in-mission all across South Asia. After twenty-one years in institutional leadership training, we were called to a very unique pastoral ministry in Kolkata—a local church which served as the hub of a Mission with a strong social outreach across East India.

One of two questions that frequently had me preoccupied and with which I often struggled in the course of my mission engagement was: How should the relationship between evangelism and social concern be expressed in a way that is both biblically sound and optimizes missional impact? While I had reflected, taught and written on this issue on previous occasions, reflecting on various sources from the perspective of my grassroots experience in preparation for the APTA lectures helped me crystallize my thoughts on this critical issue with greater clarity and confidence than ever before. I was amazed to see how the Spirit-led intuitive responses of first-generation Pentecostals, who naturally and spontaneously blended social and evangelistic engagement, anticipated the more systematic formulations of Pentecostal theologians that have emerged in recent times. Pentecostals who have a genuine experience of the Spirit have always been moved by love to share the good news of Jesus and the same Spirit moves them to extend God's compassionate concern for the poor, to feed the hungry, to reach out to the oppressed and so on.

The other question that was my constant preoccupation was: Is there anything distinctive about Pentecostal leadership training that is uniquely shaped by the Pentecostal experience of the Spirit? In other words, if there is a distinctive Pentecostal tradition that shapes Pentecostal social engagement and missiology, how does that impact Pentecostal leadership development? I believe that it should and does, and the final article in the series attempts to answer how that could happen.

I am grateful to the APTA leadership for providing the occasion for my reflection on this critical theme. I am also indebted to Dr. Dave Johnson of the APTS Press for the incentive and encouragement to publish these lectures. If they inform and bless the reader, in addition to those acknowledged in the footnotes, my thanks is also due to innumerable unnamed people whose teachings, writings and stories have shaped my reflection on the theme down through the years. To God alone be the glory!

Foreword

There are occasions, when a book comes along at a critical time, where the insights provided and foundations established through its publishing, fills a broad vacuum with new vision. Dr. Ivan Satyavrata has written just such a book at a critical moment where serious theological reflection about the Church's engagement with the poor again requires recalibration. If readers will take seriously the sturdy scholarship and prophetic voice of Dr. Satyavrata, we will avoid the debilitating results of popular pop justice causes of the day that threaten to dissipate the Church's witness with feel good activities that rob the fullest impact of Spirit-empowered ministry.

I think it is particularly appropriate that a Majority world leader would write such a theological corrective. The American propensity for the bifurcation of evangelism and social concern activities is again swinging the proverbial pendulum toward an out of balance point on the continuum. It is instructive that a Pentecostal leader, who lives in a context where Christianity is a distinct minority, is the author of such a book. With the stakes, increasingly higher, the Church must reflect Jesus fairly in word, deed and sign or cease to be a viable metanarrative. Dr. Satyavrata provides us a clear pathway to vital demonstration of the viability of the Gospel in a tragically volatile global climate.

I believe that *Pentecostals and the Poor: Reflections From the Indian Context* will become a central resource, not only for our tradition, but for a 21st century Christianity that is growing exponentially around the world and values the Spirit-empowered life and ministry. This volume's strength is focused around several critical elements: It has *missiological focus*, it is *contextually dynamic*, it exhibits *contemporary awareness*, it demonstrates *biblical and theological rootedness* and it affirms the *vitality of Pentecostal life*. Joined together, these foci yield a dynamic volume that is at once a scholarly treatise, while providing accessible inspiration to the broadest of interested readers.

Missiological focus is not the same as saying this is a book with a missions focus. Missiology is a discipline that works in the intersection of theology, social science and the history of Christian movements. It is not a function of current attempts to be *missional,* that all too often end up being so broad as to be ineffective in describing any ministry activity with particularity. Neither is it an attempt to build biblical foundations for our mission projects. Satyavrata's missiological focus demonstrates what British scholar Christopher Wright calls a "missional hermeneutic". In other words, we see the current events and trends of our world as the context in which God's redemptive activity toward all creation is unfolding. As the Church continues the mission of Jesus, we take our awareness of the world through evaluative lenses such as social science *seriously*. We see the story of God's mission through God's people in their engagement with God's work for the sake of the whole of

God's creation in the Bible **authoritatively**. *Pentecostals and the Poor* is a clear and concise example of missiology done well.

This volume is *contextually dynamic* because the author has spent a lifetime among those people who are the objects of God's redemptive concern. From being a street preacher in the poorest sections of Mumbai to leading significant ministries of compassion in Kolkata, this volume emerges from the real tragedy of humankind that is the daily experience of the author. The author acknowledges the particularity of his writing with sub-titles like *Reflections From the Indian Context*. This acknowledgement is not self-described delimitation, but affirmation of the legitimacy of the writing. This is not a book written in a conceptual vacuum, but the reflection of an author who has travailed through the volatility of humanity in its most desperate moments and settled in his heart that enduring and effective ministry to the poor must be rooted in the continuing ministry of Jesus through His Body, the Church.

This volume exhibits *contemporary awareness,* not only in its obvious interaction with contemporary events and realities. Additionally, Satyavrata demonstrates his clear identification with the moment in history that he stands, when he asks a most vital question: *What do we need to do to effectively channel our Pentecostal legacy to the next generation?* Using his long experience as evangelist, pastor, college president and renowned international scholar, the author considers the necessity of legacy. He affirms that theological education, framed for contemporary impact, is ultimately the steward of the Gospel. That stewardship includes how we interpret what was handed down to us, the strategy and tools we use to disseminate or propagate that legacy in our lifetime and how we diligently apply ourselves to ensure its authentic to future generations. This is not a contemporary awareness that flashes shocking data to attract attention. This is contemporary awareness that understands the Christian faith as an historical reality that deserves serious reflection on where it is; where we have come from; where we are at present and how we may move into the future with clear connection to redemptive events that secure our legitimacy. This book is Ivan Satyavrata's response to the necessity of channeling a Pentecostal legacy to the next generation.

Satyavrata's *biblical and theological rootedness* affirms the belief that theology must emerge from ministry activity. Theology requires our spiritual discernment of the present tense of Jesus' redemptive mission, continuing by the power of the Holy Spirit, that takes seriously participation in the messiness of human lives. In the context of humankind, that desperately needs the transforming power of Jesus Christ, the continuing work of the Spirit keeps in step with the redemptive plan of God seen most clearly in Jesus Christ. Jesus is the clearest and most complete picture of redemption humanity has ever seen and that narrative is authoritatively recorded in the Bible. Satyavrata makes obvious that the authoritative source for any Pentecostal scholar to understand the essential concept of what mission entails, is clearly the Bible. This is not an enterprise to find selected biblical texts by which to buttress one's "cause du jour" marketed for popular applause. He is quite clear that if Pentecostals are truly to represent Jesus fairly to the poor the central theme of Scripture needs to be acknowledged in its entirety. While seeing the trajectory of God's redemptive mission clearly as the central theme of the Bible, Satyavrata sees the biblical narrative of the earthly mission of Jesus as the crucible for understanding the mission of the Church to live in the reality of the rule of God represented in the Kingdom of God.

Ivan Satyavrata clearly affirms his Pentecostal identity. He demonstrates a clear awareness of Pentecostal history with an informed sense of its global texture. He offers a very thorough explanation of what it means to be part of Pentecostal tradition. However, rather than isolating his Pentecostal identity from other Christian faith traditions through a discussion of Pentecostal *distinctives*; he demonstrates the maturity of a person who is confident in the legitimacy of his faith family while implicitly acknowledging it is but one of many Christian siblings. He offers us this demonstration of Christian maturity by describing the *affirmations of the vitality of Pentecostal life*. In the current milieu of global Christianity, "distinctives" usually describe practices and emphases that a faith tradition does which sets it apart. A discussion of "affirmations" demonstrates what practices and emphases that a faith tradition places its "accent marks" on. For example, the author says that a "theologically robust Pentecostal understanding of mission thus views mission in terms of *God's ongoing redemptive project of extending his kingdom-rule to people of all nations as the Holy Spirit empowers the whole Church to take the whole gospel to the whole world.* As a Pentecostal I look at this statement and say Amen! That will preach! I also acknowledge, with just as enthusiastic an Amen, that this statement incorporates the language of the

Lausanne Covenant about the mission of the Church. That is why this book is so vital for both we who self-identify as Pentecostals and for those who can be enriched by the author's understanding of mission, though they would not call themselves Pentecostals.

I admit that my brief description of *Pentecostals and the Poor* is biased. Ivan Satyavrata has been a friend for more than 20 years. Our families are close: we have stayed for extended visits in each other's homes, though we live thousands of miles apart. We have traveled together and enjoyed close friendship that is a treasure we both hold dear. But my personal relationship with Ivan also enhances my deepest respect for the extraordinary mind and scholarship that is in full view in this volume. It is proper that reflections "from the Indian context" be instructive globally. It is time that we in the West listen to the voices of those who represent places in the world where the Gospel is most resisted and least accessible; largely because that is where followers of Jesus demonstrate a vibrant Spirit-empowered ministry that is the exemplar for 21st century Christianity.

Byron D. Klaus, President
Assemblies of God Theological Seminary, Springfield, Missouri USA, (1999-2015)

Content

iii	Publisher's Preface
v	Author's Preface
ix	Foreword
1	This is That: The Pentecostal Tradition of Social Engagement
19	Pentecost and Mission: Biblical Perspectives
37	Power to the Poor: Towards a Pentecostal Theology of Social Engagement
57	Stewarding a Legacy: The Role of Pentecostal Theological Education 2 Timothy 2:1-2

1.0 *This is That*...:
THE PENTECOSTAL TRADITION OF SOCIAL ENGAGEMENT

¹And when the day of Pentecost was fully come, they were all with one accord in one place. ²And suddenly there came a sound from heaven as of a rushing mighty wind, and it filled all the house where they were sitting. ³And there appeared unto them cloven tongues like as of fire, and it sat upon each of them. ⁴And they were all filled with the Holy Ghost, and began to speak with other tongues, as the Spirit gave them utterance. ⁵And there were dwelling at Jerusalem Jews, devout men, out of every nation under heaven. ⁶Now when this was noised abroad, the multitude came together, and were confounded, because that every man heard them speak in his own language....¹²And they were all amazed, and were in doubt, saying one to another, **What meaneth this?** *¹³Others mocking said, These men are full of new wine. ¹⁴But Peter, standing up with the eleven, lifted up his voice, and said unto them, Ye men of Judaea, and all ye that dwell at Jerusalem, be this known unto you, and hearken to my words: ¹⁵For these are not drunken, as ye suppose, seeing it is but the third hour of the day. ¹⁶But* **this is that** *which was spoken by the prophet Joel*... (Acts 2:1-6, 12-16, KJV).

How should we describe the "Pentecostal" tradition? Peter's response on the day of Pentecost began with the phrase (in King James' language): *This is that* . . . If the Pentecostal tradition has its roots anywhere, it must be in the dramatic, visible outpouring of the Holy Spirit on the Day of Pentecost as recorded in Acts 2. This is not just an internal claim, but is clearly attested by researchers outside the movement, as for instance in the recent project of Miller and Yamamori who observe:

> The major engine driving this transformation is Pentecostalism, an expression of Christianity that dates back to the first century, when the Holy Spirit is reported to have visited a small band of Jesus' followers who spoke in "other tongues" and subsequently healed the sick, prophesied, and established a network of churches throughout Asia Minor (see Acts 2).[1]

In my country of India the Pentecostal tradition has its roots in an 1860 awakening in the Tirunelveli district of Tamil Nadu in South India in the ministry of an Anglican catechist named Aroolappen. He records that " . . . some of our people praised the Lord by unknown tongues, with their interpretations. . . . Some prophesy, some speak by unknown tongues with their interpretations." Other occurrences included intense conviction of sin, conversion of unbelievers, prayer for the sick, concern for the poor, visions and people falling down under spiritual power.[2]

---

[1] Donald E. Miller and Tetsunao Yamamori, *Global Pentecostalism: The New Face of Christian Social Engagement*, 17.
[2] Gary McGee, "Pentecostal Phenomena and Revivals in India: Implications for Indigenous Church Leadership," *International Bulletin of Mission Research* (July 1996): 113.

This was followed by stirrings of revival in 1905, first in the Khasi Hills of Northeast India and then in the Mukti Mission led by Pandita Ramabai and Minnie Abrams in Western India. It then spread to other parts of India including Bombay, Madras, Kerala, Punjab, Gujarat and Bengal. Of special interest to me personally is the description of how Pentecost came to my own city of Kolkata in 1907 during revival meetings led by Azusa Street missionaries Alfred and Lillian Garr:

> The deep sense of conviction of sin resulted in people falling to the floor, howling, shrieking, groaning "as if the judgment day had already come," sobbing, writhing, shaking "as if realizing that they were sinners in the hands of an angry God," and "wails of despair . . . so heart-rending that they might have come from the regions of the damned." Other features included the frequent reading of jubilant Psalms; vocal expressions such as "Praise the Lord," "Glory to God," "Hallelujah," in addition to "holy laughter." . . . Under the inspiration of the Spirit, different voices blended creating "awe-inspiring" singing in tongues. . . . In one instance, a person even wrote in an unknown language; when holding a pen, their hand "was moved rapidly by an unseen power across the sheet [of paper], line after line [writing] Spirit-given messages which wait for interpretation." Another time, a "strong current of wind" blew through a "seekers' meeting" making it seem as if they were reliving the Day of Pentecost themselves. Sometimes solemnity reigned as believers

engaged in intercessory prayer with "groans that words cannot express" (Rom 8:26).[3]

Today over one hundred years later, I look back to a Pentecostal legacy handed down to us through such Pentecostal pioneers and missionary statespersons as Alfred and Lillian Garr, Maynard and Gladys Ketcham, Alfred and Elizabeth Cawston, Mark and Huldah Buntain and John and Faith Higgins. As I witness all the exciting things that God continues to do in the midst of all the struggles and challenges we face in the Assemblies of God (AG) work in Kolkata, I have to say again: *This is that . . . !*

When we attempt to define our Pentecostal tradition, in a sense we try to answer the same question that Peter responded to following the Pentecostal outpouring in Acts 2: *What meaneth this?* So, how should we frame our *This is that . . .*? How do we go about defining our Pentecostal tradition?

The word "tradition" has its roots in the Latin *trado/ tradere*, which means "to hand over, hand down, deliver, leave behind, impart," and commonly refers to the handing down of statements, beliefs, legends, customs, information and stories from generation to generation, especially by word of mouth or by practice. It is one of those terms which can be used in a number of different ways. It can refer to beliefs, customs and practices taught or simply passed on by one generation to the next. It can also refer to a broad religious movement made up of religious denominations or church bodies that have a common history, customs, culture, and, to some extent, body of teachings. In Judaism it refers to an

---

[3]Gary McGee, "The Calcutta Revival of 1907 and the Reformulation of Charles F. Parham's 'Bible Evidence' Doctrine," *Asian Journal of Pentecostal Studies* 6:1 (2003): 128-129.

ordinance of the oral law not in the Torah but held to have been given by God to Moses. In the Christian sense it can denote a doctrine not explicit in the Bible but held to derive from the oral teaching of Jesus and the Apostles.

When we turn to the Bible, we observe at first glance what appear to be conflicting attitudes to tradition. In Mark 7:3-13 Jesus clearly takes an adversarial posture towards the traditions to which the Pharisees and teachers of the Law gave such importance. The traditions referred to here were the oral law and written rabbinical regulations which comprised the Talmud. Jesus censures the Pharisees and teachers of the Law for allowing their traditions to supersede the express will of God. Hence, while the Talmud has academic value as a reference document, its traditions are in no way binding upon us as Christians. On the other hand Paul seems to display a positive attitude toward traditions in several of his epistles: "Therefore, brethren, stand fast, and hold the traditions which ye have been taught, whether by word, or our epistle"; and "Withdraw yourselves from every brother that walketh disorderly, and not after the traditions which he received from us" (2 Thessalonians 2:15; 3:6). The Greek term *paradosis* normally denotes oral tradition and suggests that Paul's words here probably apply to doctrinal and ethical instructions, rudimentary creeds and confessions given to churches before the New Testament writings came into existence. However, since the Reformation, Protestant churches have maintained that the writings of the New Testament alone constitute the final, trustworthy and authoritative record of the apostolic tradition, superseding all prior and subsequent oral tradition.

In a provocative work, brilliant in its theological creativity and originality, Simon Chan seeks to address what he regards as "the problem of Pentecostal traditioning." On one hand, while acknowledging that Pentecostals already do have a tradition, he simultaneously sounds a clarion call inviting Pentecostals to develop a tradition, a process which his own "traditioning" project seeks to take forward.[4] While a sustained critique of Chan's thesis is beyond the scope of this paper, this author can hardly ignore his treatment of this issue in any reference to Pentecostal tradition (especially in this part of the world) even if only to clarify my own presuppositions in this paper.

John Carpenter's rejoinder quite plainly illustrates the implicit irony in Chan's "traditioning" exercise, which rather than capturing the essence of the Pentecostal faith tradition, in effect succeeds in transforming it beyond recognition. While my own view does not coincide exactly with that of Carpenter, my essential orientation is in line with his insistence on *historical integrity* if any "traditioning" process is to be authentic: it must take into account "the actual historical tradition of the movement." As Carpenter maintains, we cannot with integrity say ". . . we are merely seeking to re-establish a tradition if we are, in reality, advocating entirely new doctrines and practices."[5] He rightly points out that while Chan speaks of "recovering" the original experience of the early Pentecostal movement, his theological strategy introduces elements such as neo-orthodoxy, Catholic mysticism, post-liberal hermeneutics and sacramen-talism, all of

---

[4]Simon Chan, *Pentecostal Theology and the Christian Spiritual Tradition* (Sheffield: Sheffield Academic Press Ltd, 2000), 20.
[5]John B. Carpenter, "Genuine Pentecostal Traditioning: Rooting Pentecostalism in its Evangelical Soil: A Reply to Simon Chan," *Asian Journal of Pentecostal Studies* 6:1 (2003): 304.

which are far removed from the history and traditions of Pentecostals.

My fundamental disagreement with both Chan and Carpenter is with a critical assumption underlying both their analyses. Both of them fall into the common error of treating Pentecostalism as though it were a single monolithic stream all over the globe. All such projects are reductionistic in assuming implicitly and somewhat simplistically that the global Pentecostal movement has a single epicenter in North America, and hence, the influences that fed into the North American Pentecostal movement are responsible for shaping all of the streams of global Pentecostalism. It is impossible to deny the fact that North American Pentecostalism has exercised massive determinative influence on the global Pentecostal movement. However, as recent studies have demonstrated repeatedly, in actual fact the Pentecostal movement is a complex blend of heterogeneous national, cultural, religious, socio-economic, theological and ecclesiastical sources and streams of influence.[6]

Andrew Walls shows that the theological challenge in gospel transmission involves holding together in tension two opposing tendencies, the "Indigenizing" principle and the "Pilgrim" principle. The "Indigenizing" principle, rooted in the fact of the incarnation, keeps converts connected with the particulars of their local culture, so that Christ and Christianity are at home in any culture. The "Pilgrim" principle, also grounded in the gospel, is the universalizing factor which critiques converts' local culture and unites them with the universal faith community, all the people

---

[6]For instance, Miller & Yamamori, *Global Pentecostalism: The New Face of Christian Social Engagement*, 19.

of God at all times everywhere.[7] As Walls shows, these principles have been operative in the missionary expansion of Christianity all through its history, but I would argue that these are especially evident in various local expressions of the Pentecostalism movement that have emerged across the globe over the last century. Thus, while there are clearly some common elements across the different local expressions of Pentecostalism, African Pentecostalism clearly bears the marks of African traditional religions, Korean Pentecostalism has a shamanistic influence, Indian Pentecostalism has been shaped by the *bhakti* religion and other distinctly Indian influences, and so on.[8]

Is there then a distinctly "Pentecostal tradition"? If so, then how do we go about distinguishing or defining this tradition? I would argue that strictly speaking there is no one Pentecostal *tradition*; what we do have is multiple Pentecostal *traditions* which bear a certain family resemblance. I am, however, prepared to employ the term in a nuanced sense within Walls' framework, which both circumscribes the unique features of this family resemblance and keeps each local tradition vitally connected to the "Pilgrim" sources of historic Christianity. We may thus speak of a Pentecostal tradition in this sense as expressing the common "Pilgrim" elements of a network of contemporary Pentecostal movements that draw their distinctive family features from the

---

[7]Andrew F. Walls, The *Missionary Movement in Christian History: Studies in the Transmission and Appropriation of Faith* (New York: Orbis, 1996), 3-9.

[8]Mathews A Ojo, "Pentecostal and Charismatic Movements in Modern Africa" in *The Wiley-Blackwell Companion to African Religions,* ed. Elias Kifon Bongmba (Oxford: Blackwell, 2012): 295-309; Amos Yong, *The Spirit Poured Out On All Flesh* (Grand Rapids: Baker Academic, 2005), 51; Ivan Satyavrata, "Contextual Perspectives on Pentecostalism as a Global Culture: A South Asian View," in *The Globalization of Pentecostalism: A Religion Made To Travel,* ed. Murray Dempster, Byron Klaus & Douglas Petersen (Oxford: Regnum, 1999), 211, 220.

Pentecostal outpouring experienced by the early disciples as recorded in Acts 2. While Pentecostal faith affirms and seeks to be firmly grounded in Scripture, a fundamental premise of Pentecostals is that the immediate, manifested presence of the Holy Spirit experienced by the early Church in Acts is normative for the Christian faith community today.

Pentecostals have thus always regarded the experience of the early Church in the Book of Acts as normative for the theology and practice of the faith community, and view their appropriation of that experience as germane to and a vital hermeneutical key in their interpretation of the Bible and understanding of the Christian faith. Consequently, the distinctive family features that mark Pentecostal movements across the globe center around a "recovery" and emphasis of the Acts 2:4 doctrine of the baptism in the Holy Spirit, understood as a normative "charismatic" experience providing empowerment for ministry; and an emphasis on spiritual gifts, especially speaking in tongues, healing and prophecy.

With this clarification of an important premise, we move on to our next task in this paper: to show that there is adequate support within the historical sources of the Pentecostal movement for a Pentecostal "tradition" of social engagement. This is especially important in the light of the perception in some quarters that Pentecostals either do not have a strong tradition of social engagement or, worse still, are altogether devoid of a social ethic or social awareness. There are two main reasons for this misconception. First, Pentecostals have been largely an oral community, and thus have not been good at documenting their experience. Second, the Pentecostal movement emerged at a time when conservative Christians as a whole were reacting to the excesses of the social gospel movement. Consequently, they did their best to distance themselves from liberal views of social concern which sought to reduce the Christian gospel to pure philanthropy. Recent studies have, however, sought to correct this misleading notion.

The Pentecostal tradition of social engagement has its roots in the work of many of the early Pentecostal pioneers, many of whom were actively involved in social transformation and works of compassion. We look first at the hallowed locations of Topeka, Kansas and Azusa Street, Los Angeles, California to where the origins of the Pentecostal movement are commonly traced. The Bethel Healing Home, which Charles F. Parham (1873-1929) started in Topeka, Kansas in 1898, enlarged its activities to include rescue missions for prostitutes and the homeless, an employment bureau and an orphanage service.[9] The relationship between love and the baptism of the Holy Spirit was very crucial to William J. Seymour (1870-1922), the leader of the Azusa Street Mission. For Seymour, the Pentecostal experience of baptism in the Spirit is about immersion in love, with ". . . the power to draw all people into one Church, irrespective of racial, ethnic or social diversity."[10] Frank Bartleman's famous one-liner summarized the impact of the Azusa Street revival, "The color line was washed away in the blood."[11]

---

[9] Gary B. McGee, "Tongues, The Bible Evidence: The Revival Legacy of Charles F. Parham," *Enrichment* (Summer 1999): n.p.

[10] Iain MacRobert, "The Black Roots of Pentecostalism," *Pentecost, Mission and Ecumenism Essays on Intercultural Theology 75* (Frankfurt am Main: Verlag Peter Lang Gmbh, 1992), 9.

[11] Frank Bartleman, *Azusa Street* (South Plainfield, NJ: Bridge Publishing, original in 1925, republished in 1980), 54.

In his *Introduction to Pentecostalism*, Allan Anderson observes:

> Pentecostals in various parts of the world have always had various programs of social action, ever since the involvement of Ramabai's Mukti Mission in India in the early 1900s and the work of Lillian Trasher among orphans in Egypt from 1911. Early Pentecostals were involved in socio-political criticism, including opposition to war, capitalism and racial discrimination. African American Pentecostals have been in the forefront of the civil rights movement. Throughout the world today Pentecostals are involved in practical ways caring for the poor and the destitute, those often "unwanted" by the larger society.[12]

According to Anderson, the Mukti revival in Kedgaon, near Pune in India, led by the famous social reformer Pandita Ramabai (1858-1922) was as much a center of pilgrimage for propagating the Pentecostal doctrine of Spirit baptism as Azusa Street was. It started in 1905, a year before the events in Los Angeles, when hundreds of young Indian women in her center were baptized by the Spirit, saw visions, fell into trances and spoke in tongues.[13] Most of these women were outcasted child-widows, who had come to Ramabai's *ashram* (community religious centre) to find shelter. The Ramabai Mukti Mission is still active today, providing housing, education, vocational training, and medical services, for

---

[12]Allan Anderson, An *Introduction to Pentecostalism* (Cambridge, UK: Cambridge University Press, 2004), 276-277.

[13]Allan Anderson, "Spreading Fires: The Globalization of Pentecostalism in the Twentieth Century," *International Bulletin of Missionary Research* (January 1, 2007): 9; See also Allan Anderson, "Pandita Ramabai, the Mukti Revival and Global Pentecostalism," *Transformation* 23/1 (January 2006): 37-48.

many needy groups including widows, orphans, and the blind[14]. She is still celebrated as a national icon of the Women's development movement in India.

In his editorial article on "Pentecostals and Social Ethics," Cecil Robeck also refers to the charity works of early Pentecostal pioneers like Stanley H. Frodsham, George and Carrie (Judd) Montgomery and A.J. Tomlinson.[15] For many Pentecostal ministries, like Gerrit Polman in the Netherlands, the Salvation Army's non-political approach of "Soup, Soap and Salvation" served as a model for their social involvement.[16]

Petersen observes that in the course of his thirty year tenure, J. Philip Hogan, former Executive Director of the Division of Foreign Mission of the Assemblies of God, frequently emphasized the commitment and active involvement of the AG in alleviating suffering through its compassionate ministries. In responding to critics on one occasion he wrote:

> We [have] invested millions of dollars and devoted countless lives to feed starving people, clothe poor people, shelter homeless people, educate children, train disadvantaged adults and provide medical care for the physically ill of all ages. We have always generously responded to the pleas of foreign nations after natural disasters, hurricanes, floods, and earthquakes. . . . I want the world to know that the reason we

---

[14]See their website Mukti Mission Home, http://www.mukti-mission.org/.

[15]Cecil M. Robeck, Jr., (Editorial), "Pentecostals and Social Ethics," *Pneuma: The Journal of the Society for Pentecostal Studies*, 9, no. 2 (Fall 1987): 105-106.

[16]Cornelis van der Laan, *Treasures Out of Darkness: Pentecostal Perspectives on Social Transformation*, Paper presented to the Symposium 'Spirit and Struggle: Beyond Polarization', Free University, Amsterdam, October 12, 2009, 2.

do these things is because Jesus did them. . . . We have no other motive than that.[17]

It is especially interesting to note that even as far back as 1980 Hogan was concerned that social relief and compassion efforts needed to be extended to social justice issues as well, "[Pentecostals] must strike at the depths of the structures of human culture and life."[18]

Support for a social engagement "tradition" may be found in the writings of the most respected AG missiologist of the previous generation, Melvin Hodges. Like most other evangelicals of his era who were concerned that the missionary mandate never be allowed to degenerate into a purely "social gospel," Hodges does warn against the tendency to any such dilution of the gospel of spiritual regeneration. However, in his *A Theology of the Church and its Mission* he is careful to spell out his conviction concerning the Church's social responsibility in the following words:

> Christians are the salt of the earth. Their presence and influence do affect society. . . . Christians by their very nature love righteousness and hate iniquity. They will, therefore, be championing every just cause and endeavoring to show "good will to all men". . . . We can do no better than follow the words of Jesus and the example of the early Christians. True Christians are a force for righteousness and social betterment. We have only to look at what is happening on the mission fields where the church has multiplied to see this process

---

[17] J.P. Hogan, *Mountain Movers,* 31, June 1989, 10-11.
[18] J.P. Hogan, *DFM Annual report of 1980*, 12.

taking place. . . . The proponents of the theology of liberation are correct in insisting that *the gospel is for the whole man and that Christians should not limit their interest to the souls of men and the future life. Christians must not be indifferent to oppression or injustice in the world* [Author italics].[19]

We need to highlight two critical features here: 1] Hodges' observation regarding the positive impact of social engagement on effective church growth in AG mission fields; 2] His appeal to this empirical data in support of his endorsement of a clearly holistic missiology. Hodges thereafter goes on to affirm both the Wheaton Declaration and Lausanne Covenant statements on Christian social responsibility before stating his own position as follows:

It is evident that evangelicals do have a concern for the whole man. Nevertheless, the spiritual need of man is given primary importance as this opens the way to all else. Evangelicals consider their task to be communicating the gospel of Jesus Christ *both by proclamation and by deed* [Author italics], thus letting their "light so shine that men can see their good works and be drawn to Christ" (cf. Matthew 5:16).[20]

We need hardly say more, but as Petersen suggests, for missionaries like Melvin Hodges who lived and worked in contexts of poverty and social oppression, and who witnessed firsthand the power of the gospel to transform every aspect of life,

---

[19]Melvin L. Hodges, *A Theology of Mission: A Pentecostal Perspective* (Springfield, MO. Gospel Publishing House, 1977), 96.
[20]Hodges, A Theology of Mission, 118.

it was next to impossible to be comfortable with any missiology that insisted on proclamation evangelism and provided no room for a Christ-like response to the social realities of pain and suffering that surrounded them. I am personally convinced that it is the intrinsically missionary nature of the Pentecostal movement that has helped shape its social conscience and resulted in the emergence of a genuine tradition of social response.

In August 2009, the General Council of the Assemblies of God, USA, responded to a strong appeal from General Superintendent George Wood and made a rare change in their Statement of Fundamental Truths, by adding "works of compassion" to the mission of the church (article 10) and ministry (article 11).[21] After the resolution was approved, Wood sought to dismiss the fear expressed by some that the Fellowship would drift toward a "social gospel" by saying, "That fear is unwarranted because evangelism and compassion feed each other when joined at the hip."[22] Article 10 includes a fourth clause that says, "To be a people who demonstrate God's love and compassion for all the world (Psalms 112:9; Galatians 2:10; 6:10; James 1:27)." The experience of the Baptism in the Holy Spirit "Enables them [believers] to respond to the full working of the Holy Spirit in expression of fruit and gifts and ministries as in New Testament times for the edifying of the body of Christ *and care for the poor and needy of the world* (Galatians 5:22-26; Matthew 25:37-40;

---

[21]Rob Cunningham, Business session focuses on resolutions, Friday, August 7, 2009, http://ag.org/top/Events/General_Council_2009/ News/20090807/20090807_01_Business.cfm (Accessed October, 1 2015).

[22]Rob Cunningham, Council wraps up business, Saturday, August 8, 2009, http://ag.org/top/Events/General_Council_2009/News/20090808/20090808_BusinessDay3.cfm (Accessed October 1, 2015).

Galatians 6:10; 1 Corinthians 14:12; Ephesians 4:11,12; 1 Corinthians 12:28; Colossians 1:29)." Clause 4 in Article 11 asserts that a divinely called and scripturally ordained ministry leads the Church in "Meeting human need with ministries of love and compassion (Psalms 112:9; Galatians 2:10; 6:10; James 1:27)." The fact that social engagement is now explicitly accepted as a fourth distinctive ministry of the Church is a significant development in the Assemblies of God.

As the Pentecostal movement has grown over the past century, its social impact has become increasingly more evident. After observing earlier that "Pentecostals are increasingly engaged in community-based social ministries," and seek "a balanced approach to evangelism and social action," Donald Miller and Tetsunao Yamamori launched a four-year field study of growing churches in the developing world that engaged in significant social ministries. Four hundred experts around the world were asked to nominate churches that satisfied four simple criteria: fast-growing; located in the developing world; with active social programs; indigenous and self-supporting. They were amazed to discover that nearly 85% of the nominated churches were Pentecostal or Charismatic.[23]

While I do not agree with the authors' somewhat artificial categorization of a so-called "Progressive" segment within Pentecostalism, a number of their conclusions are extremely helpful. In the first place, their work represents a strong validation of our claim that a concern for social engagement within the Pentecostal movement is not an innovation. They clearly affirm that there have always been Pentecostals who have sought a

---

[23]Miller and Yamamori, Global Pentacostalism, 42-43.

holistic understanding of their faith: "Throughout the history of Pentecostalism there have been examples of compassionate social service, so this is not a new phenomenon."[24] Their study also documents a wide range of types of social engagement by Pentecostals, from humanitarian responses to crises and human need (such as floods, drought and earthquakes), to education, economic development, medical work and other projects that focus on community development.[25]

Further, their empirical data indicates a wide and growing acceptance of this holistic understanding of the Christian faith within Pentecostal churches worldwide.[26] Perhaps one of their most valuable findings is the clear distinction their study observes between the Pentecostal approach to social ministries and Social Gospel or Liberation Theology frameworks of social engagement, the Pentecostal response consciously derived from Jesus' pattern of ministry:

> Unlike the Social Gospel tradition of the mainline churches, this [Pentecostal] movement seeks a balanced approach to evangelism and social action that is modeled after Jesus' example of not only preaching about the coming kingdom of God but also ministering to the physical needs of the people he encountered.[27]

Furthermore, in contrast to these older approaches, Miller and Yamamori observe that Pentecostals do not attempt to reform

---
[24]Ibid., 211-212.
[25]Ibid., 213.
[26]Ibid., 3, 212.
[27]Ibid., 212.

social structures or challenge government policies, but rather take "an incremental approach to social change by human needs that confront them on a daily basis," addressing social problems, one person at a time.[28] To that extent the Pentecostal project engages social issues at a more subversive level, attempting to construct an alternative social reality grounded on certain core kingdom values: that all human beings are made in the image of God; that all people have dignity and are equal in God's sight; and consequently have equal rights whether they are poor, women or children.[29]

It is thus no longer true or accurate to caricature Pentecostals as being "so heavenly minded that they are of no earthly use." An honest assessment of the Pentecostal tradition confirms that, for the most part, Pentecostals have not always viewed people as "souls with ears," but rather in Miller and Yamamori's words: "Instead of seeing the world as a place from which to escape, they want to make it better, especially by following Jesus, who both preached about the coming kingdom and healed people and ministered to their social needs."[30] Pentecostals today offer not only spiritual refuge from the problems of this world but concrete and authentic social engagement alternatives.[31] They have in fact done so from the very beginning as a natural extension of their evangelism and missionary efforts.

---

[28] Ibid., 216.
[29] Ibid., 4-5.
[30] Ibid., 30.
[31] Douglas Petersen, *Not by Might Nor by Power: A Pentecostal Theology of Social Concern in Latin America* (Oxford: Regnum Books International, 1996), 233; Paul N. van der Laan, "Towards a Pentecostal Theology of Compassion," *Journal of the European Pentecostal Theological Association* Volume 31, Issue 1 (April 2011): 36-52.

2.0 Pentecost and Mission:
BIBLICAL PERSPECTIVES

Half a century ago, in what has been commonly hailed as a landmark contribution to the theology of missions, Harry Boer set forth as one of the fundamental theses of his study the somewhat startling observation that "Pentecost has not played a determinative role in missionary theological thinking..." and that for the most part ". . . a missionary theology centering around Pentecost and its continuing meaning for the church has not been developed."[1]

The years since Boer made this observation have witnessed the spectacular growth of the Pentecostal movement.[2] We need hardly belabor the point, but a recent survey by the Pew Forum on Religion and Public Life estimates that the Pentecostal movement comprises one-quarter of the world's two billion Christians, making one out of every twelve people on planet Earth Pentecostal-Charismatic.[3] This growth has made Pentecostalism the most dynamic and fastest growing segment of Christianity today and on its way to becoming the predominant global form of Christianity in the twenty-first century.[4]

---

[1] Harry Boer. *Pentecost and Missions* (Grand Rapids: Eerdmans, 1961), 63.
[2] Sturla J. Stalsett, ed., Spirits of Globalization: The Growth of Pentecostalism and Experiential Spiritualities in a Global Age (London: SCM Press, 2007), 1.
[3] A decade and a half earlier, Peter Wagner had made this astute observation: "My research has led me to make this bold statement: In all human history, no other non-political, non-militaristic, voluntary human movement has grown as rapidly as the Pentecostal-Charismatic movement in the last 25 years." Vinson Synan, *The Spirit Said "Grow,"* Innovations in Mission 4 (Monrovia, CA: MARC, 1992), ii.
[4] This is no longer just an observation made by Pentecostals themselves or even Christian missiologists; Robbins provides an excellent summary review of the anthropological and other

With this growth has come widespread interest in the place of Pentecost and the role of the Holy Spirit in mission.

Where does a Pentecostal theologian begin when trying to understand a concept as essential to biblical faith as mission? The first place to begin is the Bible of course! The obvious difficulty, however, is that neither the term "mission(s)" nor "missionary" is to be found in our English Bible. For the first fifteen centuries of its history, the Church used the Latin term *missio* in theology to refer to the "sending" of the Son by the Father, and the "sending" of the Holy Spirit by the Father and the Son. What we today refer to as "mission(s)" was referred to by phrases such as "preaching of the gospel," "propagation of the faith," "extending the reign of Christ" or "planting the church." It was only during the colonial era that the Jesuits began to employ the term "mission" to denote the spread of the Christian faith among those outside the Church. From then on "mission(s)" has come to be used to refer to the means by which the Church fulfills Christ's mission in our world.[5]

If the term "mission(s)" is not to be found in the Bible, how may we arrive at a biblically sound understanding of the concept? The difficulty with definition arises not from the lack of adequate biblical terminology as much as the richness and breadth of biblical teaching on the subject, which Christians today have tried to capture in the all-encompassing term "mission(s)." As Bosch observes, while no single overarching term for mission exists in the New Testament, the New Testament uses close to one hundred Greek expressions which have a direct bearing on a biblical understanding of mission.[6] The Bible is

---

scholarly literature dealing with the global spread and impact of Pentecostalism, Joel Robbins, "The Globalization of Pentecostal and Charismatic Christianity," *Annual Review of Anthropology* 33 (October 2004): 117-143.

[5]David J. Bosch, *Transforming Mission: Paradigm Shifts in Theology of Mission*. American Society of Missiology Series. No. 16 (New York: Orbis, 1991), 1.

[6]Bosch, *Transforming Mission*, 16.

thus the *original* handbook on mission(s), and any attempt to derive a definition of "mission(s)" exclusively from a few select terms, or from one or two preferred scripture texts is bound to lead us to a truncated and deficient understanding of "mission(s)." The theme is too critical, too central to the purpose of God for us to limit the fullness of its biblical scope and vision.

The Kingdom of God and the Mission of Jesus

How may we take Bosch's caution to heart in trying to arrive at a truly biblical understanding of mission in a short monograph of this nature? A safe starting point would appear to be the life and ministry of Jesus and to view the Church's mission as a continuation of the mission of Jesus. The basis for this is clearly set forth in the fourth Gospel in at least two places: "As you sent me into the world, I have sent them into the world," and again " . . . As the Father has sent me, I am sending you" (John 17:18; 20:21).[7] Bishop Leslie Newbigin reminds us of the crucial significance of the little word *"as"* in the Johannine version of the Great Commission in the following words "It is the manner in which the Father sent the Son that determines the manner in which the Church is sent by Jesus. Its mission is governed by the manner of his."[8] Our understanding of "being sent" should thus be modeled after Jesus' manner of "being sent." His way of mission should determine the way we understand and carry out mission. Jesus, in turn, sends His disciples "as the Father sent him."

The Gospels clearly teach that God acted decisively to fulfill his redemptive purpose in Jesus Christ and the kingdom of God has

---

[7]John Stott also shows a preference for the Johannine version of the Great Commission, Leslie Newbigin, *Mission in Christ's Way* (Geneva: WCC Publication, 1987), 23; cf. John Stott, *Christian Mission and the Modern World* (London: Falcon Books, 1975), 23.
[8]Newbigin, *Mission in Christ's Way*, 23.

arrived and become a present reality in his life and work. The kingdom of God is, however, both a present reality and a promise which awaits future fulfillment. The kingdom of God has already broken into history and is present among men and women in great power in the person of Jesus. Although the new age has been inaugurated in Christ, the consummation of the new age still remains in the future.

Jesus' mission on earth was thus inseparably connected to the kingdom of God and consisted essentially in making known and manifesting the reality of the kingdom. The words and works of Jesus were directed toward a clear end and purpose: extending the kingdom-rule of God in the hearts of people.[9] The concept of the kingdom is central to a biblical understanding of mission and the Church's mission can only be rightly understood in the light of the kingdom of God. While the theme is rich both in terms of biblical content and is also the subject of much theological discourse and varied interpretation, there are three crucial aspects to Jesus' teaching on the kingdom that have bearing on our understanding of mission.

1) Announcement of the Kingdom's Arrival

At the outset of his mission "Jesus went into Galilee, proclaiming the good news of God. 'The time has come,' he said. 'The kingdom of God is near. Repent and believe the good news!'" (Mark 1:14-15). Newbigin uses the term "news-flash" to describe this verbal witness to the arrival of the kingdom. This is the prophetic dimension of mission. Something new has happened: the kingdom-reign of God has come near and this fact must be announced.[10]

---

[9] C. Rene Padilla, *Mission between the Times* (Grand Rapids: Eerdmans, 1985), 186-189.
[10] Newbigin, *Mission in Christ's Way*, 1.

2) Demonstration of the Kingdom's Reality

Two of the Synoptic Gospels record an incident in which John the Baptist sends some of his disciples to Jesus seeking some sort of confirmation concerning Jesus' Messiahship. Luke notes that Jesus performed a number of miracles of healing and exorcism in their presence and then replied, "Go back and report to John what you have seen and heard: The blind receive sight, the lame walk, those who have leprosy are cured, the deaf hear, the dead are raised, and the good news is preached to the poor" (Luke 7:22 cf. Matt.11:4-5).

It is difficult to miss the indissoluble link between deeds and words in the life and ministry of Jesus as recorded for us in the four Gospels. The mission charge given to the Twelve in the tenth chapter of Matthew begins with a commission merely to heal the sick and exorcise demons. The charge to preach the message of the kingdom only comes later in verse 7 of the same chapter. Preaching, on this occasion at least, seems to have constituted an explanation of the works of healing. Although the works of Jesus and the apostles did not by themselves communicate the new fact of the kingdom, they were vital demonstrations of the reality of the kingdom.[11] Newbigin explains the significance of the close link between the miraculous acts and words of Jesus as follows:

> In the Gospels the new reality is the presence of Jesus himself. He is here. In him the kingdom of God has come near so that it now confronts men and women with its reality. . . . The presence of that new reality is attested by the mighty works of Jesus, which in

---

[11]Leslie Newbigin, *The Gospel in a Pluralist Society* (Grand Rapids: Eerdmans, 1989), 132.

turn call for the explanation which is the preaching of the gospel of the kingdom.[12]

3) Extension of God's Kingdom-Rule

This is an aspect of mission that raises the most number of questions: How does God extend his kingdom-rule? What does it involve? Is it simply a matter of "saving souls?" We are right in saying that God's kingdom-rule is extended every time an unbeliever repents and accepts Christ as Lord and are most closely acquainted with this aspect of the saving work of Christ. On the cross of Calvary Christ paid the penalty and made atonement for the sins of all those who would believe in him. Those who believe in him are justified by grace through faith, have their sins forgiven and partake of eternal life (2Cor.5:21; Eph. 2:8-9; 1Pet.2:24). Jesus, however, commanded his disciples not just to "save souls", but to "***make disciples*** . . . of all nations" (Matt 28:19-20). What does this involve?

Unfortunately we have too often restricted our under-standing of discipleship to a narrow individualistic view of personal holiness, based on a truncated understanding of what was accomplished in the penal-substitution atonement of Christ. So while we taught people that following Jesus means that we get baptized, are filled with the Spirit, attend church, give to God regularly, make an honest living, take care of our families and be good neighbors, we failed to nurture them to develop a kingdom-shaped worldview. So we have Spirit-filled believers and churches displaying un-Christian attitudes toward slavery, racism, casteism; insensitivity toward issues of poverty,

---

[12]Ibid., 133.

economic exploitation, social oppression and human suffering in general.

There is a deep need to capture the holistic implications of Christ's atoning death based on a more robust anthropology and harmartiology. If sin has affected every aspect of man's being, Christ redeemed us from every dimension of the curse when he bore our sins on the cross of Calvary. The benefits of Christ's death, thus, have a bearing on every aspect of the human personality. While the new life we receive in Christ makes us primarily new creatures through spiritual regeneration, this life must overflow and affect physical, mental and emotional health, as well as restore dignity and wholeness to human life and society lost through the Fall. True discipleship thus involves submitting every area of our lives to the lordship of Christ, a process which continues to extend the reign of God within the lives of individual followers of Christ and the community of believers as a whole.

The Holy Spirit and Mission

At Pentecost the Holy Spirit took up his dwelling place in the Church as he ushered in the new age. The presence of the Spirit in the Church is clearly an eschatological phenomenon. A characteristic feature of the period at the end of the age is the presence of the Spirit, and the central function of the Spirit during this period is the bestowal of life. Not only is the life of the Church derived from the poured-out Spirit, the life of the Church finds her central expression in *witness* to the crucified and risen Lord. There is thus an indissoluble relationship between Pentecost and the missionary witness of the church. "It is at *Pentecost* that the witness of the church began, and it is *in the power of the Pentecostal Spirit* that this witness continues to be carried forward." [Author's italics][13] Pentecost made the church a witnessing church, and her witness was spontaneous, immediate, effective and directed to ever widening circles of men.

When we consider the Holy Spirit's role in the mission of Jesus, we see that the Spirit was intimately associated with the life and ministry of Christ from start to finish. He supernaturally superintended the miracle of the incarnation in the womb of Mary. Jesus' ministry was inaugurated by the Holy Spirit at his water baptism. Luke records how Jesus returned from the Temptation in the wilderness in the power of the Spirit, and in the synagogue at Nazareth on the Sabbath, stood up and read from the scroll of Isaiah, "The Spirit of the Lord is on me, because he anointed me . . ."(Luke 4:18-19). We see Jesus' mission thereafter led and controlled at every stage by the Holy Spirit.

It was by the Spirit's power that Jesus demonstrated the power of God and the reality of the kingdom in his mighty miracles of healing and exorcism (Matt. 12:18, 24-32; Mk. 3:22-30). It was by the Spirit that Jesus surrendered himself in substitution for sinners at the cross, and by the Spirit he was raised from the dead (Heb. 9:14; Rom. 8:11). When Jesus was challenged by the Pharisees regarding the source of his authority and power he responded, "If Satan drives out Satan, he is divided against himself. How then can his kingdom stand? . . . But if I drive out demons by the Spirit of God, then the kingdom of God has come upon you" (Matt. 12:26, 28). The New Testament account of Jesus' life and ministry makes best sense when set against this backdrop of a real but invisible conflict between two kingdoms—the kingdom of God and the kingdom of this world or the ruler/prince of this world, Satan.

---

[13]Boer. *Pentecost and Missions*, 87.

Following the coming of the Spirit and the birth of the Church on the Day of Pentecost, the Church has continued to be engaged in constant spiritual warfare with the principalities and powers of evil in the world (Eph. 6:11-12). The world system in which evil is organized against God imposes on mankind a lifestyle of bondage to the principalities and powers of evil. The gospel is the good news of Jesus Christ's victory over the powers of evil (Col. 2:15; Heb. 2:14-15). The gospel, thus, offers not only reconciliation with God through Jesus Christ, but also a transformed lifestyle under the rule of God. Padilla points out that the Church has only two alternatives in its encounter with the world, " . . . either it adapts itself to the world and betrays the gospel, or it responds to the gospel and enters into conflict with the world."[14]

The Holy Spirit's role in mission must thus be viewed in the light of this conflict between the kingdom of God and the powers of evil which are at cross-purposes with it. It is the Holy Spirit who provides the people of God with the power needed for spiritual resistance against the idolatrous, enslaving and destructive activity of the powers of evil (Luke 10:18-19; 24:48-49; Acts 1:8). The Holy Spirit thus impacts every aspect of the Church's mission, a mission by which *the whole church takes the whole gospel to the whole world.* The following is but one framework by which we can outline the Spirit's role in this regard.

1) Intercession

"Your kingdom come, your will be done on earth as it is in heaven. . . ." (Matt. 6:10). Undergirding all of the Church's missionary efforts is a two-fold conviction. First, the realization that at the root of the

---

[14] C. Rene Padilla, *Mission between the Times* [Grand Rapids: Eerdmans, 1985], 58.

missionary enterprise is a cosmic spiritual warfare in which the kingdom of God through the Church is pitted against the principalities and powers which are under the control of "the prince of this world" (Jn. 12:31; Eph. 6:12). In a number of places the New Testament makes reference to the *archai* and *exousiai* which dwell "in the heavenly realms" (Eph. 1:20-21; 3:10; 6:12; Col.1:16; 2:15).[15] Paul describes how Christ's death on the cross has rendered a mortal blow to the principalities and powers which manipulate individuals blinded and taken captive by Satan, as well as the demonic structures which perpetuate evil in society,"And having disarmed the powers and authorities, he made a public spectacle of them, triumphing over them by the cross" (Col.2:15).

Second, is the conviction that although God is sovereign and in total control of the affairs of the universe, he has entrusted us with a vital key for seeing his kingdom established on the earth. It is in this context that we need to recognize the Spirit's crucial role in mission to empower the Church to confront the cosmic forces of evil through Spirit-energized prayer and intercession (Rom.8:26-27; Eph. 6:18). The powers of darkness must be engaged in combat through spiritual intercession at every level. The influence of evil in the lives of individuals, in the Church, and in social and political structures must be resisted and the victory of Christ enforced in the power of the Spirit (Mark 9:29; Eph.6:19-20; Col. 4:12; 1 Thess. 5:17; 1 Tim, 2:1-2).

---

[15]In his commentary on Ephesians, John Stott argues convincingly that interpreted in the context of the NT world-view shared by Jesus and the early church, the term "principalities and powers" seems most naturally to denote supernatural powers or beings who inhabit the unseen world of spiritual reality. Although he hesitates to equate these "powers and authorities" with human structures, institutions and traditions, he does allow for the real possibility that these "personal supernatural agencies" can use structures, traditions and institutions as well as people in their opposition to the kingdom purposes of God.

2) Proclamation

The arrival of the kingdom must be announced, but as Paul points out, "The god of this age has blinded the minds of unbelievers, so that they cannot see the light of the gospel . . ." (2 Cor. 4:4). The prophetic spirit anoints representatives of the kingdom and empowers them to *preach* and *proclaim* that the kingdom has arrived in Christ (Luke 4:18a; Acts 4:29, 31).

This gospel must be proclaimed "in the whole world . . . to all nations" (Matt 24:14; cf. 28:19; Mark 16:15). This is where the emphasis on reaching unreached people groups and the call to prioritize the "apostolic function" of missions finds its place.[16] The good news, the announcement that the kingdom has arrived in Christ, this "newsflash" must go out: *Jesus saves . . . spread the news to every land . . . the 'earth' must hear his voice!*

3) Demonstration

The kingdom must not only be announced, its reality must be demonstrated "in power." Paul thus declares to the Corinthians, "My message and my preaching were not with wise and persuasive words, but with a demonstration of the spirit's power, so that your faith might . . . rest . . . on God's power" (1 Cor.2:4-5).

In Acts 1:8 Jesus promised that his disciples would receive *power* when the Spirit came upon them and they would *be* his witnesses. While the Book of Acts is filled with instances of dramatic "power-encounters" such as supernatural healings, exorcisms and other

---

[16] See Alan Johnson, *Apostolic Function in 21st Century Missions* (Pasadena: William Carey Library, 2009).

miraculous signs, the radical nature of the *koinonia,* love and unity, experienced by the early church equally demonstrated "in power," the reality of the kingdom's presence in their midst (Acts 3:6-10; 5:12-16; 2:42-47; 4:32-37). The Spirit's empowerment of the Church thus equips the Church with the power to manifest the kingdom's real presence through "signs" of the kingdom that confirms the Church's claims and provide authenticity to her witness.

4) Reconciliation

The kingdom extends its influence as unbelievers are drawn into the fellowship by the Holy Spirit. Spirit-led intercession first loosens and breaks the hold the evil one has on unbelieving minds; they then hear an anointed proclamation of the gospel message confirmed by some demonstration of the Spirit's powerful witness to the reality of the kingdom's presence. This is how the people of God are empowered by the Spirit to exercise their "ministry of reconciliation", inviting people on Christ's behalf to "Be reconciled to God . . . " (2 Cor. 5:20).

Those without Christ who are *"dead [author's italics]* in transgressions and sins" (Eph.2:1; Rom.5:12), need a radical work of the Holy Spirit in order to be reconciled to God through the atoning work of Christ on the cross. The Holy Spirit first *convicts* (John 16:8-10) and then *regenerates,* implanting the divine nature within the heart of the repentant sinner (Jn.1:13; 3:3-8; 1 Pet. 1:23). He then works powerfully to create new life, releasing the sinner from his bondage to Satan and communicating a new nature that eventually affects every aspect of his personality and life-style (2 Cor.5: 17; Eph.2: 5, 6; 1 Pet.1: 3).

5) Social Transformation

A theology professor, Antoine Rutayisire from Rwanda, shared the following case study in the course of a moving presentation on the theme of "Reconciliation" at the Lausanne conference in Cape Town in October 2010. Christianity in Rwanda experienced spectacular growth in the early half of the twentieth century. By 1941 the king of Rwanda was baptized. All the chiefs and influential personalities followed suit, making Rwanda the epitome of a fulfilled dream. In the early 1930's, a mighty revival broke out setting the Eastern Africa countries on fire and reaching even beyond. Uganda, Tanzania, Kenya, Burundi and other countries still celebrate the fruit of that mighty revival. However, between 1959 and 1963 the cradle of the revival was rocked by a bloody ethnic massacre. While the church kept growing and was working hand in hand with the government, discriminatory policies were put in place and even complied with by the churches. The general population census of 1991 showed that Rwanda had a Christian population of 89%. Between 1990-1994 ethnic tensions intensified greatly, eventually resulting in a horrible genocide in 1994 in which more than one million people were brutally massacred, often inside church buildings, and in many cases, with the participation of clergy members.

We live in a world that has been marred by the effect of sin. Individual sin overflows into the social and political structures of our world resulting in all kinds of political oppression, economic exploitation, social evil and injustice (such as hunger, poverty, human trafficking, racism, casteism), disease epidemics and natural disasters—all of which call for a Christian response. As the "salt of the earth" and the "light of the world, the *sign* and *agent* of God's kingdom in the world," the Church must also actively resist these forces of evil which hold sway in society.

In Ephesians chapter 2, Paul outlines the New Testament kingdom vision of a single new humanity based upon Christ's atoning work on the cross (Eph. 2:14-16). This is but one aspect of the breadth of the kingdom mission's holistic scope, which looks forward to "a new heavens and a new earth," a vision which only has credibility if God's kingdom people are engaged in meaningful social transformation in the present.

The Pentecostal Church-in-Mission

What are the implications of all that we have looked at thus far for the Spirit-empowered Church? Our first assertion is that mission is properly *Missio Dei*—mission is about God and God's kingdom. God is bringing his kingdom in, and we are invited to participate in the process. In Chris Wright's comprehensive missional biblical theology based on his careful application of a missional hermeneutic to the message of the Bible as a whole, he argues strongly for the theological priority of God's mission. "Fundamentally, our mission (if it is biblically informed and validated) means our committed participation as God's people, at God's invitation and command, in God's own mission within the history of God's world for the redemption of God's creation."[17] Wright argues that it is misleading to take our missiological starting point only from the human activities of mission, however biblical, Spirit-directed, and important they may

---

[17]Christopher J. H. Wright, *The Mission of God: Unlocking the Bible's Grand Narrative* (Downers Grove, IL: InterVarsity Press, 2006), 23.

be. God is on mission, and all humanly-initiated mission or missions flow from the prior and larger priority of the mission of God.[18]

Mission is thus not primarily a human enterprise; it is the outworking of God's sovereign, eternal purpose and plan for his world. It is important to emphasize this especially in a day and age when technology, education, media, funding strategy, and marketing seem to have become indispensable to the work of missions.[19] God's mission must never degenerate into a humanly-engineered, corporate marketing enterprise. From start to finish it must always remain a God-dependent, Spirit-empowered, Christ-glorifying endeavor.

Second, if the Church is called to co-operate in the Mission of God, and to continue and complete the mission of Christ on the earth, how are we to interpret the Church's mission? Our review of the biblical teaching through the grid of Jesus' understanding of his mission illustrates its multifaceted nature. A series of processes are involved in taking the gospel to the various peoples of the world and presenting it in a way that they can respond to meaningfully. The actual task of "mission(s)" today thus entails recruitment and training of workers; their administrative, financial and pastoral support; research into unreached people groups/mission fields; language acquisition and translation work; evangelistic activity; compassionate ministry/development work that authenticates verbal witness; discipling and nurture; church-planting; and training of workers/ministerial education.

---

[18] Most Bible-believing Christians would agree that the Bible provides a basis for mission. Chris Wright believes that there is actually a missional basis for the whole Bible—it is generated by, and is all about, God's mission; Wright, 531.

[19] Al Johnson cites evangelical sociologist John Seel's scathing critique of evangelicalism's uncritical accommodation, before adding his own solemn word of caution: "When we scratch beneath the surface of our rhetoric about the leading of the Spirit and spiritual dynamics we find ourselves to be part of a system. . . .Thus, we believe that more money and better technology will solve our problems. . . . As we pursue the efficient production of results based on our market driven indicators of success our agendas supersede all else, while those we purportedly come to serve become the tools that we utilize to achieve our ends, Johnson, *Apostolic Function*, 221.

Disagreement and debate sometimes arises over whether "mission(s)" should properly be restricted to all or only some of those aspects referred to above.[20] Thus, in contemporary usage, a distinction has sometimes been made between "mission"—its broader biblical and theological sense, and "missions"—a more restricted reference to the more specific cross-cultural missionary ventures. In addressing this dilemma, Bosch, on one hand, recalls Stephen Neill's famous words, "If everything is mission, nothing is mission," in cautioning against the tendency to define mission too broadly. On the other hand, he warns against "straight-jacketing" what is in reality "a multifaceted ministry" by "any attempt at delineating mission too sharply."[21] Bosch's wise conclusion reminds us that the truth in this case, as in many other aspects of biblical precept and practice, lies in the balance between two extremes.

The issue is less about terminology than about biblical integrity and theological consistency. For drawing too deep a distinction between "mission" and "missions" runs the risk of distancing the Church from mission—of separating, and in some cases "legitimizing" the Church's "non-missional" activities from its "missional" activities, including its cross-cultural mission mandate. A truly Pentecostal ecclesiology, however, always views the Church as the Church-in-mission, and a truly Pentecostal missiology refuses to see mission apart from the life of the Church. The Church and mission are thus organically related as root to the fruit, and any understanding of one which does not include the other will result in an inadequate

---

[20] The term "mission(s)" today is thus used in a wide variety of ways. In the opening page of Bosch's classic work on mission, he lists no less than twelve conventional uses, and in the course of his extended treatment introduces a wide range of contemporary applications of the term, especially focused in his discussion of thirteen paradigms in chapter 12; Bosch, 1, 368-510.
[21] Ibid., 511-512.

view of both.[22] Hence, all that the Church does—its worship, discipleship and church growth, salt and light living, evangelism, church planting, and cross-cultural missions—should be intentionally directed toward extending the kingdom of God on the earth.[23]

Two important clarifications are necessary. First, the concern that a broader definition of mission runs the risk of the term losing its cutting edge when it is inflated to include everything that the Church does. When the Church *is* the Church as Jesus intended it to be, it should be a Church-in-Mission, and must not engage in any activity that does not in some way further God's kingdom-mission. The counter argument is that, in actual fact, the Church often does not do what it should, and hence every activity it engages in cannot be called mission. The difficulty with this objection is that it derives legitimacy implicitly from deviant contemporary social expressions and practices of the Church rather than from the biblical vision. A constricted understanding thus poses an even greater danger to "apostolic" mission in that by distancing Church from mission it deepens and legitimizes the divide between the Church's routine non-missional activity and the specialist "mission" activity.

Second, a broader understanding of mission in no way undermines the strategic priority of cross-cultural mission and church planting among unreached people groups. Rather, it seeks to provide theological legitimacy and motivation for broader participation in the Church's cross-cultural missionary enterprise. Hence, rather than seeing mission as the responsibility of a privileged few with an apostolic calling and gifting, it envisions mission(s) as an enterprise in

---

[22] A point stressed in Emil Brunner's famous saying: "The Church exists by mission as a fire exists by burning", quoted in Wilbert R. Shenk, *Write the Vision* (Harrisburg, PA: Trinity Press, 1995), 87.

[23] A. Scott Moreau, Gary R. Corwin, and Gary B. McGee, *Introducing World Missions: A Biblical, Historical, and Practical Survey* (Grand Rapids: Baker, 2004), 77-79.

which the whole body of Christ is actively involved: the researcher whose work assists the church planter; the health or development worker whose motivation is to authenticate the gospel message so that unbelievers will be drawn to Christ; the educator who helps equip missionaries for the mission field; the pastor who nurtures a missions-giving and missions-sending church; and the mission official who administers, mentors, and cares for the needs of missionaries.[24]

Conclusion

The Church is, thus, called to continue the mission of Christ. In the footsteps of Christ, the Church must continue to announce the arrival of the kingdom, demonstrate the reality of the kingdom in her life and seek to extend the influence of the kingdom in the hearts of men and in human society. It does so by enforcing the victory wrought by Christ on the cross over the powers of evil which actively resist the kingdom-extending purposes of God. The Holy Spirit enables the Church to be a Church-in-Mission, making mission an enterprise in which the whole Church is engaged intentionally and instrumentally, The Holy Spirit is also a filter that orients and directs every activity of the Church toward the extension of the kingdom. A theologically robust Pentecostal understanding of mission thus views mission in terms of *God's ongoing redemptive project of extending his kingdom-rule to people of all nations as the Holy Spirit empowers the whole Church to take the whole gospel to the whole world.*

---

[24]To use a military metaphor, the various functions of the Church are to "missions" what the armament factory, corps of engineers, military training camps, and supply lines are to the front-line of the battle. Each have a different function, but all are equally soldiers in the same army, fighting for the same cause, at war with the same enemy.

3.0 Power to the Poor:
TOWARDS A PENTECOSTAL THEOLOGY OF SOCIAL ENGAGEMENT

The extraordinary success of the Pentecostal movement is largely due to its outreach to those on the periphery of society. Some see the reasons for this success as due to sociological factors; others see it in essentially the "power" factor associated with the Holy Spirit's dynamic empowerment. The Pentecostal message is very good news among the poor; it answers their immediate felt needs and provides powerful spiritual impetus and community support for a better life. Several recent studies have shown that the intervention of Pentecostal mission into severely deprived communities unleashes powerful redemptive forces resulting in upward social mobility of believers. The genius of Pentecostalism has thus been its relevance to the powerless—its ability to penetrate the enslaving power structures of the socially and economically marginalized.

Although Pentecostals have from their outset been deeply involved in works of compassion, they have in general been better at doing it than articulating it in statements of faith or theological formulations. Thus Doug Petersen, writing just over a decade ago, laments the fact that despite the substantial contribution of the Assemblies of God to social involvement, "a certain 'gap' exists between pragmatic compassionate outreach and an adequate understanding of biblical foundations which must guide these actions."[1] Petersen's own work in this area has contributed significantly towards bridging this gap.

Dr. George O. Wood, Chairman of the World Assemblies of God Fellowship and General Superintendent of the Assemblies of God, USA, observes, "It's probably been the nature of the Pentecostal experience that we have the experience first and then develop the rationale!"[2] A statement issued at the conclusion of the European Pentecostal Theological Association on the theme "Pentecostals and Justice" in July 2010, observed the following:

> We agree that our heritage as Pentecostals demonstrates a profound concern for works of mercy, justice and compassion for the poor and that the Full Gospel that we have historically proclaimed addresses the whole range of human need, be it spiritual, physical or social. However, we recognize that we have only of late rediscovered the implications of what that means in terms of our holistic mission to the world.[3]

There were, however, some features of Pentecostal belief and practice which mitigated a proper theology of social engagement, most of which were a carry-over from the fundamentalist antecedents of many early Pentecostals. Some reasons why social

---

[1] Douglas Petersen, "Missions in the Twenty-First Century: Toward a Methodology of Pentecostal Compassion," *Transformation* 16:2 (April 1999]: 54.
[2] George O. Wood, *Letter to Dr. Joseph Dimitrov*, March 29, 2010
[3] EPTA Statement on Pentecostals and Justice, Mattersey Hall College and Graduate School, England (July 9, 2010].

action was not prominent on the theological radar of Pentecostals were:[4]

1. Millennial eschatology - Pentecostals came at a time when "evangelicals" didn't have time to think about building the kingdom of God, because of their conviction of the imminent return of Christ and the shift towards a pre-millennial position. Apocalyptic doomsday scenarios with the inevitable impetus towards "otherworldliness" leave little room for concern about social engagement.
2. The rise of old liberalism and the social gospel tended to taint Pentecostal, Holiness, and Evangelical involvement with issues of social justice. As Pentecostals rubbed shoulders with Evangelicals they also adopted the values and concerns of Evangelicals who stood against the liberals who employed the social gospel.
3. Dualism – Again in reaction to reductionist tendencies in modernist versions of Christian mission which highlighted this-worldly, physical benefits of the gospel, Pentecostals sought to give priority to the salvation of the "soul."
4. Apolitical posture – Pentecostals seemed reluctant to integrate anything in their doctrinal statements that seemed politically tainted. Both the Assemblies of God and the Church of God (Cleveland) for instance took a strong pacifistic position during World War I, though

---

[4]Cecil M. Robek, Jr., (Editorial), Pentecostals and Social Ethics, *Pneuma: The Journal of the Society for Pentecostal Studies*, Volume 9:2. (Fall 1987): 106.

not explicitly expressed in their statement of faiths developed during those very turbulent years.

Other challenges included the impact of the prosperity gospel which, by postulating almost a *karma* like cause-effect relationship between faith and material wealth, implied that the poor deserve their status. Furthermore, concern for practical social needs was commonly viewed by Pentecostals as a natural inseparable part of evangelism, and hence they never felt the need to develop a distinct theology for it. A final observation worth noting in this regard is that as a revival movement, Pentecostalism was in general less concerned about developing theology than it was about seeing the Holy Spirit infuse the Church with spiritual vibrancy and a burden for world evangelization. The limited theological concerns of Pentecostals were thus devoted to providing biblical justification of their distinctive doctrinal emphasis on the baptism in the Holy Spirit and related teachings. While there is no denying the fact that, especially in the early stages of the movement, the urgency to evangelize tended to blur the vision for social justice, right from the beginning Pentecostals have also excelled in various kinds of social programs.[5]

Whatever the reasons for the lack of adequate articulation of a theology of social concern, it is impossible to deny that social engagement is today an essential component of the Pentecostal missionary movement in most regions of the world. As an astute researcher observes, ". . . engagement in social ministry by

---

[5] Velli Matti, Kärkkäinen "Spirituality and Social Justice."

Pentecostals has practically exploded in the last few decades."[6] But is this a welcome development? Is this the result of the Holy Spirit's leading or something that Pentecostals have wandered into inadvertently? How firmly is this trend anchored in Scripture? When Pentecostals embrace this heightened emphasis on social engagement, are they being faithful to the roots of their tradition or are they merely yielding to cultural pressures?

Whether or not we agree with those who would view this as an unhealthy trend, the questions raised are not only valid, but vital for the future of the movement, and highlight the need for us to develop a cogent and cohesive Pentecostal theology of social engagement. A task of this nature is necessarily both communal and cumulative: *communal* because it has to emerge from an ongoing conversation within the global Pentecostal community; and consequently *cumulative*, because it must bring together perspectives that reflect the various contextual Spirit-illuminated readings of Scripture and the actual experience and praxis of Pentecostal reflective practitioners in different regions of the world. What follows must be viewed as a modest contribution to this ongoing conversation.

Our strategy in outlining a theology of social engagement both builds on the two earlier presentations and carries it forward. To begin with, we must ensure that our theology emerges from, and is in close alignment with, the clear teaching of Scripture. "If this engagement of social responsibility exists as a legitimate expression of Pentecostal ministry, then it must reflect biblical

---

[6]Kent Duncan, "Emerging Engagement: The Growing Social Conscience of Pentecostalism," *Encounter: Journal for Pentecostal Ministry* 7 (Summer 2010): 2.

roots and align with sound biblical doctrine."[7] Our consideration of the biblical material which shapes our understanding of Pentecostal mission in the previous lecture has helped us lay a foundation for this.

Secondly, although Scripture is our final authority in any theological formulation, it helps our case if we can draw corroborative support from the testimony of history. A robust theological formulation will explore the sources of Christian tradition and glean what it can from the insights of the fathers of the faith. The witness of those who lived closest to the apostolic era is especially helpful in this regard.

Thirdly, we focus on the distinctive theological resources of the Pentecostal movement itself, in particular, Pentecostal spirituality. Pentecostal theological thinking and action springs from a transforming spiritual experience (a distinctive second work of the Spirit), usually evidenced by speaking in tongues, given for an endowment of spiritual "power" for witness and/or to be active participants in God's mighty works. This experience provides a sense of the nearness and redemptive power of God's Spirit break into our life today. We evaluate briefly how this Pentecostal experience helps shape the Pentecostal social conscience and social engagement.

---

[7]Duncan, "Emerging Engagement," 4

A Biblically Rooted Social Ethic

The Genesis account of creation is designed to show among other things that humankind was the climax of God's creation program. In the first recorded encounter between God and Adam and Eve in Genesis 1:28, God blesses their existence and defines their role in creation. The following two verses describe God's provision for them and all living creatures. This means that God's first word to human beings is a word of direction; the second word is a word of provision, indicating God's intention that all of humankind are provided for in their journey of life. Poverty is thus a contradiction of God's primary intention that the basic living needs of all of humanity are properly provided for. Both Old and New Testaments clearly support this assertion that God in his providence seeks the subsistence and survival of all his creatures (Ps 104; Ex 16; Matt 6:32-33; Acts 14:17). Hence, poverty is not in itself a blessing; it contradicts God's primary intention of providence.

Murray Dempster summarizes the Old Testament (OT) basis for a Christian social ethics in three convincing arguments.[8] In the first place he argues that Christian theological reflection must be grounded in God's self-revelation of himself and his character. God reveals himself repeatedly and unmistakably in the OT as a God who is especially concerned with the needs of the poor and the powerless, and may even be viewed as possessing a "preferential" bias for the poor against the rich. Secondly, the biblical concept of the *Imago Dei* obliges us to value all human

---

[8]Murray W. Dempster, "Pentecostal Social Concern and the Biblical Mandate of Social Justice," *Pneuma: The Journal of the Society for Pentecostal Studies*, Volume 9:2. (Fall 1987): 130-137.

beings as created in the image of God. Our social ethic should thus flow out of our desire to treat with respect and dignity all other human beings who are also made in the image of God.

Thirdly, the unilateral Sinai covenant between God and Israel indicates that God is not merely concerned about our salvation, but also with the well-being of his creation. The Ten Commandments show that a right relation with God (Ex. 20:3-11) should be complemented by a right relationship with people in society (Ex. 20:12-17). The law and the covenant were a prescription of what life should look like for the people of God. The ministry of the prophets reminded God's people of what it means to live according to his character. Israel's socio-ethical actions were to thus demonstrate God's nature and character. God's covenant people were chosen to reflect who God is and what he does.

The nation of Israel was thus explicitly commanded by God to imitate God's special concern for the poor and oppressed (Ex. 22:21-24; Deut. 10:17-18; 15:13-15). This command is echoed in the New Testament (NT) in Jesus' teaching to his followers to imitate God's mercy and kindness (Luke 6:33-36), as well as in apostolic instructions to the Church to give generously to the needy (1 John 3:16-18), as evidence of authentic Christian discipleship (James 1:27). Not only that, the Bible also expressly warns God's people against neglect or mistreatment of the poor and the oppressed, in OT prophetic admonitions (Isa. 1:10-17; 58:3-7; Amos 5:21-24) as well as NT exhortations (Luke 1:46-53; 4:18; 6:20-25; Mark 12:38-40; James 5:1-6).

Jesus and the poor were, of course, inseparable. The needy flocked around him everywhere he went: the beggars, the sick, the destitute, the bereaved, the hungry masses, and he was always touched by their needs. Ten times the NT records that Jesus was "moved with compassion," and each time it was when he was confronted with suffering people. We have already looked briefly at Jesus' teaching concerning the kingdom of God, which is the unifying theme that provides a description of what life would look like under God's redemptive kingdom reign. Firmly within the tradition of the prophets, Jesus teaches and embodies through his parables and miracles, what life in the kingdom should look like— a life marked by justice, mercy, love, and peace.

The kingdom, the central theological concept used by Luke in his gospel to describe Jesus' mission and ministry, is the connective between the Luke-Acts account. "Those things which Jesus began to do and teach . . ." (Acts 1:1) both summarizes his earthly ministry and sets the agenda for the ministry of the apostles subsequent to their receiving the transfer of the Spirit. In effect the kingdom mission of Jesus (including his kingdom ethic) is transferred to the charismatic community by the descent of the Spirit at Pentecost. The kingdom ethic of Jesus is made operational within the charismatic community by the empowerment of the Holy Spirit and becomes thereafter the moral foundation for the life of the early church.

The Holy Spirit is presented in the Acts as one who empowers the Church to overcome the entrenched gender, economic, cultural, and religious barriers of a divided world. The book of Acts mentions two immediate results of the outpouring of the Holy Spirit on the Day of Pentecost. First, "many wonders and miraculous signs were done by the apostles" (2:43); and second, "All the believers were together and had everything in common.

Selling their possessions and goods, they gave to anyone as he had need" (2:44-45). This is further elaborated in Acts 4:32-35:

> *All the believers were one in heart and mind. No one claimed that any of his possessions was his own, but they shared everything they had. With great power the apostles continued to testify to the resurrection of the Lord Jesus, and much grace was upon them all. There were no needy persons among them. For from time to time those who owned lands or houses sold them, brought the money from the sales and put it at the apostles' feet, and it was distributed to anyone as he had need.*

In Acts 2, the *gender* distinctions of male and female were overcome by the empowerment of the Spirit. Also in Acts 2 but detailed further in Acts 4 and 5, the *economic* distinctions between rich and poor were overcome in the economic *koinonia* established by the power of the Spirit. In Acts 10, the *cultural* distinctions between Jew and Gentile were overcome within the Christian community by the coming of the Spirit. Acts 9:36 refers to the disciple Tabitha from Joppa ". . . who was always doing good and helping the poor." When the prophet Agabus predicted a devastating famine, "The disciples, each according to his ability, decided to provide help for the brothers living in Judea" (Acts 11:29). The Book of Acts demonstrates that the preaching of the gospel resulted in a loving community, where they felt responsible to meet both spiritual and material needs.

This finds resonance in the rest of the New Testament. In his letter to the Galatians, Paul mentions that the one thing which the apostles asked him and Barnabas to do as they ministered to the Gentiles was that "... we should continue to remember the poor" (Gal. 2:10). In his closing remarks he admonishes the Galatians, "Let us do good to all people, especially to those who belong to the family of believers" (Gal. 6:10). Paul's instructions to Titus also have "good works" as a central theme and concludes with the exhortation, "Our people must learn to devote themselves to doing what is good, in order to provide for urgent needs and not live unproductive lives" (Titus 3:14; cf. 2:7; 3:8). James is very explicit in his appeal to demonstrate our faith by good works, when he states, "faith by itself, if it is not accompanied by action, is dead" (James 2:17), and "to look after orphans and widows in their distress" as a mark of a "pure and faultless religion" (James 1:27). In his letters, John interprets compassion as the practical translation of God's love, "If anyone has material possessions and sees his brother in need but has no pity on him, how can the love of God be in him? Dear children, let us not love with words or tongue but with actions and in truth" (1 John 3:17-18).

The full significance of the NT Church's appropriation of the kingdom ethic of Jesus must not be diluted. Its purpose was to confirm the validity of the claim that the gospel had the power to institute in the practice of the believing community the kingdom ethic of Jesus, which fulfilled the Old Testament proclamation for social justice to reign. This establishment of a just community governed by the Holy Spirit is used apologetically by Luke to demonstrate that the Church was established by the exalted Jesus Christ (Acts 2:33, 4:32-37, 10:24-48). The Church's social ethic and engagement is thus not merely a helpful appendage to the Church's witness, but an essential and integral part of it. The

Church's social witness, in fact, authenticates its verbal witness—works and wonders must always complement word.

A Historically Attested Social Conscience

A detailed treatment is beyond the scope of this paper, but the following illustrations should suffice as evidence that the Church's social conscience remained active through the early years of its history. Justin Martyr wrote in 151 AD:

> And they who are well to do, and willing, give what each thinks fit; and what is collected is deposited with the president, who succors the orphans and widows and those who, through sickness or any other cause, are in want, and those who are in bonds and the strangers sojourning among us, and in a word takes care of all who are in need.[9]

A few decades later in 195 AD Tertullian observes in his *Apologeticus*:

> Though we have our treasure-chest, it is not made up of purchase-money, as of a religion that has its price. On the monthly day, if he likes, each puts in a small donation; but only if it be his pleasure, and only if he be able: for there is no compulsion; all is voluntary. These gifts are, as it were, piety's deposit fund. For they are not taken thence and spent on

---

[9] Justin Martyr, The Fist Apology – Chapter 67: http://www.ccel.org/ccel/schaff/anf01.viii.ii.lxvii.html (Accessed September 26, 2015).

feasts, and drinking-bouts, and eating-houses, but to support and bury poor people, to supply the wants of boys and girls destitute of means and parents, and of old persons confined now to the house; such, too, as have suffered shipwreck; and if there happen to be any in the mines, or banished to the islands, or shut up in the prisons, for nothing but their fidelity to the cause of God's Church, they become the nurslings of their confession.[10]

In his classic treatment of *The Mission and Expansion of Christianity in the First Three Centuries,* researched over a century ago, Adolf Harnack meticulously documented the works of charity of the early church. Harnack was convinced that the early church's social witness was a critical factor which contributed to its extraordinary growth. Harnack categorizes his profuse references from early church sources into ten areas of social involvement:

1. Alms in general, and their connection with the cultus and officials of the church.
2. The support of teachers and officials.
3. The support of widows and orphans.
4. The support of the sick, the infirm, and the disabled.
5. The care of prisoners and people languishing in the mines.
6. The care of poor people needing burial, and of the dead in general.

---

[10] Tertutllian, *Apology,* Chapter 39: http://www.newadvent.org/fathers/0301.htm (Accessed September 26, 2015).

7. The care of slaves.
8. The care of those visited by great calamities.
9. The churches furnishing work, and insisting upon work.
10. The care of brethren on a journey (hospitality), and of churches in poverty or any peril.[11]

Harnack's work is a gold-mine of research both for its wealth of detail and the breadth of insights it offers into the social witness of the early church. For our purpose it offers indisputable evidence that an active social conscience and earnest social engagement was a vital feature of the Church's life through the earliest years of its existence.

A Socially Transforming Spirituality[12]

The main distinguishing mark of Pentecostalism is its spirituality. The theme of the Holy Spirit's empowerment has always been at the heart of Pentecostal belief: "But you will receive power when the Holy Spirit comes on you; and you will be my witnesses . . . " (Acts1:8)

---

[11] Adolf Harnack, The *Mission and Expansion of Christianity in the First Three Centuries*, 1908, trans. by James Moffatt, 154-190: http://www.preteristarchive,cin. Books/1908_harnack_expansion. html (Accessed September 26, 2015).

[12] Murray A. Dempster, Byron D. Klaus, and Douglas Petersen, eds., *Called and Empowered: Global Mission of Pentecostal Perspective* (Peabody: Hendrickson Publishers, 1991); Eldin Villafañe, "The Politics of the Spirit: Reflections on a Theology of Social Transformation for the Twenty-First Century," 1996 Presidential Address, *Pneuma: The Journal of the Society for Pentecostal Studies*, vol. 18 (Fall 1996): 161-170; Cecil M. Robeck Jr., "Pentecostals and Social Ethics," *Pneuma*, vol. 9 (Fall 1987): 103-107; Richard J. Mouw, "Life in the Spirit in an Unjust World," *Pneuma*, vol. 9 (Fall 1987):109-128; and Murray W. Dempster, "Pentecostal Social Concern and the Biblical Mandate of Social Justice," *Pneuma*, vol. 9 (Fall 1987): 129-153.

Spirituality—living the life of the Holy Spirit—energizes and enables the Church to witness to the kingdom through evangelization and social engagement. The believer's encounter with the Holy Spirit results in a spiritual transformation that reshapes her moral and social conscious- ness, causing her to become an instrument of social change. Transformed people are empowered by the Spirit to transform the world in the light of the in-breaking kingdom of God. We will examine how Pentecostal spirituality shapes Pentecostalism's social response as we look at five key features of Pentecostal spirituality.

Prayer/Worship

Individual and corporate prayer and worship experience is a very important feature of Pentecostal spirituality. We have already observed (in our previous lecture) the critical role of prayer in missionary engagement of the powers of evil that hinder the advance of the kingdom. Prayer is in actuality the "cry" of the kingdom in response to Jesus' exhortation to his disciples to pray for the coming of the kingdom (Matt 6:10).

God's kingdom by its very nature is God's gift and work. Believers do not construct the kingdom, but rather ask for it and welcome it. It comes by grace and grows within us by the power of the Spirit. Prayer empowers us and compels us to strive for just and loving relationships among people, in family, in community, and in society. The corporate worship experience of Pentecostals is a crucial element in the shaping of Pentecostal spirituality and is a crucial stage in social engagement when directed towards kingdom advancement and in opposition to the powers of evil.

Liberation

The Pentecostal experience of Spirit baptism is basically one of empowerment, and the overwhelming reality that this experience opens to believers is liberation from captivity to the powers of evil that keep them from fullness of life. Pentecostals have always understood the empowering of the Holy Spirit as the power "to be" and the power "to do." It is liberating to those existing in the shadows, marginalized from the economic and social center of society, to those whose experience of poverty leaves them feeling helpless and disempowered. Frighteningly powerful and destructive forces that hold the poor captive must yield to the power of the Holy Spirit.

The liberating experience of the power of the Holy Spirit counters the negative experience of power as an inescapable descending spiral. The gifts of the Spirit empower their recipients "to do" and "to be," negating the significance of popular prerequisites to power, education, wealth and other status symbols. Pentecostals place high value on giftedness and spiritual power. Those who are of no consequence outside of the Church find themselves part of a rapidly growing alternative society in which they are highly esteemed and appreciated because of their giftedness. This experience of liberating empowerment has become the basis for the upward mobility of Pentecostals in society.

Healing

The belief and practice of divine healing has been a vital component of Pentecostal spirituality since the movement's inception and the earliest indisputable pointer to its holistic concern. This is one area in which Pentecostals departed early from the theology of their evangelical and fundamentalist predecessors when they sought to apply the benefits of the atonement of Christ to the whole person—body, soul and spirit. This is one reason why Pentecostals have tended to naturally and easily been moved to respond to the felt physical needs of the poor. It was impossible to believe that God's "real presence" manifested through the power of the Spirit could miraculously heal sick bodies and not want his people to care and respond to the felt physical and social needs of the poor and dispossessed.

Community

One of the signs of the Holy Spirit's empowering presence is *Koinonia*. The word *Koinonia* occurs 18 times in the NT and denotes *that fellowship among believers which the Holy Spirit creates* (2 Cor. 13:14; Phil 2:1). The *Koinonia* of the Holy Spirit involved a sharing of a common life within the Church (Acts 2:42-46; 5:42) and is illustrated in its description as the Body of Christ (1 Cor 12). This means that the members of the Body have an obligation within the Body to *"one another,"* and these obligations constitute hall-marks of *Koinonia*, marks or signs of the distinctive kingdom lifestyle, such as love, unity, justice, healing, godliness and other gifts and fruit of the Spirit.

The *Koinonia* of the Spirit enables the Church to demonstrate what the reign of God is like, to incarnate the values of the kingdom that Jesus taught. Thus "witnessing" was not something the Church did; it was a function that flowed out of the common life and experience of the Church-as-community. The early church communities did not act from a concept of social justice. The concern they showed for the poor, widows and strangers, was not a separate activity, but rather an extension of their worship and witness.

Spirit-inspired *Koinonia* at the local level has been a powerful agent of social transformation since the beginning of the Pentecostal movement. The strong sense of community, patterned after the model of the early church helps Pentecostals find a new sense of dignity and purpose in life. The *Koinonia* experience of the early Pentecostals resulted in the emergence of communities which functioned as social alternatives that protested against oppressive structures. Their solidarity created affective ties, giving them a sense of equality, and causing them to challenge inequality in the treatment of minorities, women, and the poor. During a time when racial and gender inequality was endemic, Pentecostals welcomed black and white, male and female, rich and poor.

Hope

Pentecostals view their experience of the Spirit in eschatological terms, offering a present foretaste of a promised future (Eph 1:14). Pentecostals believe that they have been called by God in the "last days" (Acts 2:17) to be Christ-like witnesses in the power of the Spirit. The hope in the imminent coming of the Lord has sustained Pentecostals during persecution, harassment, imprisonment and martyrdom during the last century. They have consistently taught that the Church must be ready for the coming of the Lord by means of faithful witness and holy living. Pentecostals today continue to believe that intense hope has been and will continue to be necessary for endurance, healing and engagement of the forces—both social and spiritual—which oppress and violate people.

A common popular understanding of future events presumes the annihilation of the world, and clearly undermines the need for sustained social engagement. But as Kärkkäinen points out, for many Pentecostals eschatological hope has brought with it optimism about the work they are doing to bring about social transformation. They view their efforts as visible "signposts," evidence that the kingdom of God has pressed into the present.[13] Miroslav Volf adds further theological validity to this position on the basis of Rom 8:21 that the liberation of creation cannot occur through its destruction but only through its transformation. He argues that kingdom oriented social projects have eschatological significance, and eschatological continuity between God's present reign and the reign to come "guarantees that noble human efforts will not be wasted."

When such eschatological continuity is postulated Pentecostal social engagement takes on different significance with fresh potential for sustaining an enduring vision of eternity as articulated in the words of a leading Pentecostal social ethicist, "Expressions of Christian social concern that are kingdom-

---

[13] Petersen, Pentecostal Compassion, 57

signifying deeds of anticipatory transformation are the kinds of human effort that God preserves, sanctifies and directs teleologically toward the future age of God's redemptive reign."[14]

---

[14]Murray W. Dempster, "Christian Social Concern in Pentecostal Perspective" (Presidential address, conference of the Society for Pentecostal Studies, Lakeland, Florida, November 7–9, 1991), 36.

4.0 Stewarding a Legacy:
THE ROLE OF PENTECOSTAL THEOLOGICAL EDUCATION 2 Tim. 2:1-2

Pentecostalism has, by its democratization of religious life, promise of physical and social healing, compassion for the socially alienated and practice of Spirit empowerment, shown that it has the essential ingredients of a social movement that can reshape the painfully harsh social reality for millions of poor and marginalized in our world. The spiritual power and hope that the Gospel of Christ infuses within the poor and deprived not only provides satisfaction for their present felt needs, it also fulfills their deepest aspirations for a brighter future.

In this concluding lecture we will need to consider the impact of what we have looked at thus far upon the critical role of theological education (TE), for which I would like to employ the motif of "legacy." At the end of thirteen years as a student in formal programs of study in four institutions and twenty-two years on the other side of the lectern—a total of thirty five years—I am convinced that at the end of the day, TE has to do with our faithful stewardship of the Gospel: how we interpret what was handed down to us, the strategy and tools we use to disseminate or propagate it within our lifetime, and how diligently we apply ourselves to ensure its authenticity as we transmit it to future generations. The question in focus today is simply: ***What do we need to do to effectively channel our Pentecostal legacy to the next generation?***

2 Timothy 2:1-2 illustrates for us how this legacy is transmitted. Paul entrusts Timothy not just with the Gospel message, but with the stewardship of the message's transmission to others. I have often used a quote that says, "An inheritance is something you leave for our kids, and a legacy is something you leave in them."[1] This statement perhaps best captures how Paul viewed his responsibility towards Timothy, Titus and other "sons" in the faith. How can Pentecostal TE most effectively help shape the Pentecostal Church and Mission in the second decade of the twenty-first century and beyond and help steward our Pentecostal legacy for future generations, should Jesus tarry?

The Vision and Goal of Theological Education

In a rapidly changing world we need to do some radical rethinking on how we presently do TE. As winds of change blow over the Church and the world today, almost everything that was once taken for granted is being questioned, and rightly so. What do we need to prepare effective leaders for the 21st century Church? Who should be trained? Should the efforts of TE be focused so much on "full-time" ministerial candidates? Are existing systems and institutions the most effective way of training leaders? Is the traditional one-size-fits-all approach to training leadership suited for the complex and specialized ministry

---

[1] Tim Elmore, *Nurturing the Leader Within Your Child* (Nashville: Thomas Nelson, 2001), 9.

demands of ministry in the 21st century? The disillusionment in many quarters of the Church and mission with traditional residential institution-based methods has resulted in the emergence of effective non-formal and informal training programs. While we cannot explore all of these issues at this time, it is important that we clarify the understanding of TE presupposed in this paper before we go any further.

The task of TE is understood in various ways, including: a) To train men and women for leadership in the Church; b) To prepare all the people of God for the work of Christian ministry; c) To educate men and women to be Christ's disciples. I would like to describe TE simply as the Church's mandate to disciple God's people, further their growth in vocational giftedness and maturity in Christ, and thus equip them to fulfill the kingdom-mission of Christ. This definition either includes or presupposes the following:

> TE is for all the people of God. This follows from the original reformation vision and flows as a logical theological consequence of the Pentecostal revival with the Spirit being poured out upon all believers, not just the "clergy."

> TE must thus be vocationally diversified and strategically layered to include every level of leadership and ministry in the Body of Christ.

> TE should never be viewed in isolation from the Church and Mission; rather it must be intentionally designed to equip the Church-in-Mission for effective verbal and social witness. It must thus be continually evaluated in relation to its

effectiveness in furthering the kingdom-mission of the Church.

TE can only affect this through holistic transformation—it must inform the mind, shape attitudes and character, enable the development of skills, transmit vision and passion, transform the whole person.

Theological Education for Transformation

What follows must be viewed as a sketch rather than a blueprint, but the four factors should be seen as pivotal in shaping of TE programs at all levels that profess to be Pentecostal. For Pentecostal TE to be truly transformative, these four areas must be carefully designed to be used by the Holy Spirit for life-transforming impact.

1) Transforming Spiritual Passion

The heart of our Pentecostal legacy is spiritual passion: a life that is regularly nurtured by the Spirit through the study of the Word and prayer, the evidence is a vibrant devotional life seen in godly character and creative fervor in ministry and mission.

Several years ago, while I was still a young theological student, a teacher and friend whom I deeply respect and admire presented me with a little book, Helmut Thielicke's A *Little Exercise for Young Theologians*. This is an introductory course for theology students which warns them of some common pitfalls of theological education and offers guidance on how to get the best from it. The climax of this great theologian's argument is a contrast he draws between sacred theology and diabolical theology. For him the contrast is not between orthodox and heretical theology. Sacred theology is "a theology which is prayed and has spiritual life";[2] diabolical theology, on the other hand, is a theology, which is spiritually barren, "a coat of armor which crushes us and in which we freeze to death."[3] His conclusion: "Whoever ceases to be a man of the spirit automatically furthers a false theology, even if in thought it is pure [and] orthodox... [for] an orthodox theologian can be spiritually dead."[4] His essential point is one which every true Pentecostal should lay hold of unquestioningly; a theology without spiritual passion is a false theology!

The call and compulsion for the ministry begins with a divine encounter (Exodus 3:7-10). Pentecostal TE too must begin where mission begins—through an encounter with God. This transforming encounter then becomes the foundation of an ongoing relationship with God. Education should lead to a deeper knowledge of God and a true knowledge of God that is marked by genuine godliness, a clearer vision of God and his purposes, the ultimate evidence of which is godly character (Mic. 6:8; 2 Cor. 3:18). The passion that the Holy Spirit ignites is not just neutral intellectual or emotional energy—it is holy passion—it will produce a transformed life—a godly life! Pentecostal TE should help produce leaders with spiritual passion, whose Christian discipleship is consequently marked by genuine godliness.

---

[2] Helmut Thielicke, *A Little Exercise for Young Theologians* (Grand Rapids: Eerdmans, 1962), 25.
[3] Ibid.
[4] Ibid.

Pentecostal TE helps foster intimacy with God, the motivator of genuine compassion for those in need, and dependence on God, the source of supernatural provision. Holistic spiritual formation, in the sense of a healthy appropriation of Christ's kingdom principles to all of life, is thus fundamental to TE for transformation. The Pentecostal impetus for social involvement flows out of an essential commitment to the Lordship of Christ and obedience to his commands to feed the hungry, clothe the naked, visit the prisoner, work for justice and empower the powerless. Pentecostal missional concern and social engagement thus has its origin in the heart of God. God sends the Christian worker as his representative to the poor and oppressed, to communicate his concern and to act on his behalf. This is a distinguishing mark of Christian social concern and it is derived from God's posture towards the oppressed and powerless.

2) Transforming Theological Formation

Helmut Thielicke's advice to theological students in Germany was that a vigorous spiritual life is an essential foundation of theological study! But growth in the knowledge of God is dependent on growth in knowledge about God. Our knowledge of God is thus informed and shaped by biblical and theological reflection. What the Bible teaches about God and the ways of God inform us intellectually, but also shape our attitudes and the way we live. Our worldviews are reshaped and transformed by our engagement with the Scriptures. But, as we know, Scripture is susceptible to various interpretations. With the emergence of post-modern hermeneutics, it is important to clarify the factors that condition the reading of those engaging social issues from a position of commitment to the authority of Scripture.

Furthermore, the pursuit of knowledge and the pursuit of truth are not the same thing. For instance, discovering an effective way of triggering a destructive nuclear device may expand the frontiers of knowledge and could perhaps in theory be a more difficult problem than a cure for AIDS. But the two discoveries cannot be compared in value. The TE enterprise needs to confront a quantitatively different but qualitatively comparable issue that often lies buried within the hallowed recesses of theological institutions, in curriculum and syllabi, text-books, examination answer scripts and dissertations. We sometimes refer to the absurdity of medieval theologians debating the question of how many angels could rest on a pin. But much of what we deal with in formal TE settings may seem as remote from the perspective of the real issues facing the average Christian worker today.

Some years ago I came across a study that was a serious eye-opener to me even though the location of the research was North America. The author of this study, Tim Dearborn presented his findings in an article entitled *Preparing New Leaders for the Church of the Future*, an evaluation of the impact of theological education on church and mission in the North American context. Dearborn's study involved interviewing hundreds of people within three constituencies: laypersons, pastors, and Bible College professors, all of who were asked to comment on the qualities of a good pastor?[5] The divergences in the order of priorities were interesting, but two illustrations should suffice to make the point.

---

[5]Tim Dearborn, "Preparing New Leaders for the Church of the Future," *Transformation* 12: 4 (1995): 7.

The quality of "Spirituality" that was given the highest priority was rated fourth by pastors themselves, but did not figure at all in the priorities listed by Bible college professors. On the other hand, "Theological knowledge" rated first by Bible college professors came fifth on the list of six for both laypersons and pastors. Dearborn's research leads him to make the following observation:

> . . . Many people emerge from seminary less equipped for ministry than they entered. Eager students entrust three years of their lives to a seminary in order to be better equipped to love God, people and the world with all their hearts, soul, strength and mind. Yet too often they graduate feeling spiritually cold, theologically confused, biblically uncertain, relationally calloused and professionally unprepared.[6]

He goes on to offer the serious indictment of TE that it is woefully out of touch with the needs of the Church, consequently leading to visionless churches and directionless leaders. His conclusion: "Finally, the heart of theological education . . . like the heart of life, is worship. We are seeking transformation for passion. Life in Christ, and . . . in ministry only does honor to God if it is a love affair. . . . Education which does not help us grow to be better lovers is heretical and indeed, blasphemous."[7]

The tough question every theology student and teacher should constantly be interrogating himself/herself with is, "How is my higher education journey affecting my relationship with God, my character, my family and other relationships?" Knowledge is

---

[6] Ibid.
[7] Ibid., 12.

power and power without character is highly dangerous. The real danger is that we may find ourselves like the emperor who thought he had an impressive new set of clothes, when in reality he had nothing on. We must not be afraid to ask the tough question, "How is the new set of 'clothes' I am acquiring through my higher education experience affecting my Christian discipleship?"

Our hermeneutical strategy and approach to biblical and theological formation should help shape sound Pentecostal scholarship based on an unflinching confidence in the transforming power of the Word of God. But our theology should also be shaped by the real issues emerging from our witness to the Gospel and its engagement with the real world. How effectively have TE graduates been equipped to respond to such questions as: What does the Bible have to say to the exploited Christian Sex Worker (CSW) in Mumbai's red-light district who has come to Christ but still continues to ply her trade because she has no other means of feeding her children? What does the Bible teach concerning the Christian response to terrorism or genocide? How can we explain the theology of "conversion" to a Hindu or Buddhist colleague at work whose anger has been provoked by the insensitive pronouncements of the Pentecostal tele-evangelist who claims to have converted tens of thousands of Hindu/Buddhist heathens at his last crusade?

Pentecostal TE cannot be only a matter of fulfilling formal academic criteria, culminating with successful performance in examinations. True biblical and theological formation must transform the mind and heart, and ultimately make a difference to the world.

3) Transforming Community

Modern leadership theory only confirms what the New Testament simply assumes (1 Cor. 4:16; Phil. 4:9), that deep and lasting change takes place not through what we teach in words; transforming influence is exercised through what the teacher/leader models through his example. Jesus' way of teaching for transformation was to model the transformed life. After washing his disciples' feet, he effectively says in John 13:14-15, "I have shown you the way it should be done; now you do it!" We keep saying it; Jesus said do it! Technology has helped us find new ways of telling the story—and we say it clearer and louder with little effect, whereas Jesus says live it!

Transforming Community Context

Real transformation can only take place within the context of a network of loving relationships, enabling an experience of genuine Christian community, either within the Church or the TE institution. Community is an essential building block of God's plan and purpose. Christian community/church serves as a sign of the kingdom. It is also the primary crucible of God's dealings with his people.

All human development takes place within the context of relationships—and at the end of the day, leadership is all about relationships—relationships that inspire and motivate others to great exploits, selfless commitment and sacrificial service. The Bible is full of such leaders.

In a seminal book on leadership, **Primal Leadership**, Boyatzis, Goleman and McKee use neurological and sociological research to show how positive emotions play a critical role in a leader's ability to lead effectively. They insist that at its root the primal job of leadership is emotional and thus requires leaders to possess high EI (emotional intelligence).[8] The roots of the idea of EI can be traced to the concept of SI (social intelligence) coined by Thorndike long ago, to refer to the ability to understand others and "act wisely in human relations."[9] In **Primal Leadership** EI is seen as the ability to inspire, arouse passion and enthusiasm—to keep people committed and motivated—to create resonance, and a key factor in producing **resonant relationships**—relationships marked by honesty, trust, commitment, compassion, loyalty, respect, humility, etc. Effective leaders are viewed as those who succeed in building resonant relationships with those around them.[10] A sequel to **Primal Leadership** entitled **Resonant Leadership** was published by two of the authors—a "how to" book in which they offer tools to help leaders create resonance in their relationships, teams and organizations.[11]

Our purpose here is not to discuss *Resonant Leadership* principles but simply to illustrate how modern leadership research simply confirms the qualities which the Bible regards as essential

---

[8] Daniel Goleman, Richard Boyatzis & Annie McGee, *Unleashing the Power of Emotional Intelligence* (Boston: Harvard Business School Press, 2004), n.p.
[9] Edward L. Thorndike, "Intelligence and Its Uses," *Harper's Magazine* (January 1920): 228.
[10] Goleman, Boyatzis & McGee, *Emotional Intelligence*, 29-52.
[11] Richard Boyatzis & Annie McKee, *Resonant Leadership* (Boston: Harvard Business School Press, 2005).

marks of good leadership. Social concern must thus be expressed within the context of the transforming community before it flows out into the world. The community is thus the most critical non-formal catalyst for transformation in the TE process. "If your actions inspire others to dream more, learn more, do more and become more, you are a leader" - John Quincy Adams.[12]

4) Transforming Mission

One of my former students was planting a church in one of the most unreached areas of the world, North India. I quote from his letter[13] a few months after his graduation: "This is a small city . . . this is the most religious group of people that I have come across. At 4:00 a.m. the temples start their sessions, and it goes on for a minimum of two hours. In the evening the temples begin their sessions again. Most of the nights they have full night sessions . . . ."

In the same letter, he states:

What am I doing here? I believe the Lord has brought me here on a specific mission with his strategy. My time here is invested in prayer, Bible Study and working on my Hindi. Most of the days, my day begins way before 4:00 a.m. The Lord by His grace has been teaching me how to pray. My time invested here is in Prayer, Prayer and much Prayer. . . . This is what I learnt: The more I pray and stay in the presence of God . . . the more the Holy Spirit controls me.

---

[12]Karen D. Bowerman & Montgomery Van Wart, *The Business of Leadership: An Introduction* (New York: Routledge, 2011), 3.

[13]Private letter to the author dated November 2, 1999.

Good theology is theology that emerges as the by-product of mission. So also, the most effective TE takes place "in-mission." Word and event always went hand in hand in the ministry of Jesus. Ivory-tower, insular, monastic models of learning must thus give way to models that try to integrate worship, word and work. The authentic and credible theologies of mission are those forged in the furnace of living engagement with issues on the mission field, rather than formulated in the classroom or library. Mission without spiritual passion is unsustainable!

Theological institutions today are, by and large, not doing a bad job of fulfilling what they are best designed to do. Professors and scholars do a good job of producing competent professors and scholars. The problem is with the design, not with the failure or inefficiency of the system. If we want to produce ministers who are effectively engaging missiological issues, students must be exposed to effective models of Christian mission. In practical terms this means that the training institution must work more closely with the Church, the academy must move into the real world. Also practitioners must be equal partners with the professors for the effectiveness of the TE process. TE must be shaped by practical engagement with the real issues, which emerge in the context of kingdom-mission involvement in the world.

A recurring issue in some quarters of relevance to theological formation as it relates to mission is what should have priority—our verbal or social witness?

The Priority of Verbal or Social Witness

Are evangelism and social responsibility of equal importance, or should one take precedence over the other? This has been a burning question that is a common topic of controversy and, at least in my view, of much fruitless debate. It helps to clarify the issue if we look at the threefold relationship between the two.[14]

First, social concern is a **consequence** of evangelism. Evangelism is the means by which God brings people to new birth, and their new life manifests itself in the service of others. Paul wrote that "faith works through love" (Gal. 5:6). James wrote, "I will show you my faith by my works" (James 2:18), and John stated that God's love within us will overflow in serving our needy brothers and sisters (1 John 3:16-18). As Robert E. Speer wrote about the Gospel in 1900, "wherever it goes, it plants in the hearts of men forces that produce new lives; it plants in communities of men forces that create new social combinations."[15]

Social responsibility is more than the consequence of evangelism; it is also one of its principal aims. For Christ gave himself for us not only "to redeem us from all iniquity" but also "to purify for himself a people of his own who are zealous for good deeds" (Tit. 2:14). Through the Gospel we are "created in Christ Jesus for good works which God prepared beforehand, that we

---

[14]John Stott, ed. *Evangelism and Social Responsibility: An Evangelical Commitment*, Lausanne Occasional Paper No. 21 (Lausanne Committee for World Evangelization, 1982), http://www.lausanne.org/all-documents/lop-21.html (Accessed on 29 October 2009); cf. Samuel Escobar, *The New Global Mission: The Gospel from Everywhere to Everyone*. Christian Doctrine in Global Perspective series (Downers Grove, Ill: IVP, 2003), 152-154.

[15]John Piper, *Robert E. Speer: Prophet of the American Church* (Louisville, KY: Geneva Press, 2000), 236.

should walk in them" (Eph. 2: 10). Good works cannot save, but they are an indispensable evidence of salvation (James 2:14-26). Social responsibility, like evangelism, should therefore be included in the teaching ministry of the church.

Second, social activity can be a **bridge** to evangelism. It can break down prejudice and suspicion, open closed doors, and gain a hearing for the Gospel. Jesus himself often performed works of mercy before proclaiming the Good News of the kingdom. Further, by seeking to serve people, it is possible to move from their "felt needs" to their deeper need concerning their relationship with God. We must serve people out of genuine love and integrity ensuring that our motives are pure, so that our actions are not perceived as bribes but bridges—bridges of love to the world.

Third, social activity not only follows evangelism as its consequence and aim, and precedes it as its bridge, but also accompanies it as its **partner**. Evangelism and social responsibility are like the two blades of a pair of scissors or the two wings of a bird. This partnership is clearly seen in the public ministry of Jesus, who not only preached the Gospel but fed the hungry and healed the sick. In his ministry, *kerygma* (proclamation) and *diakonia* (service) went hand in hand. His words explained his works, and his works dramatized his words. Both were expressions of his compassion for people. Likewise, if we proclaim the Good News of God's love, we must manifest his love in caring for the needy. Indeed, so close is this link between proclaiming and serving that they actually overlap.

To proclaim Jesus as Lord and Savior (evangelism) has *social* implications, since it summons people to repent of social as well as personal sins, and to live a new life of righteousness and peace. Likewise, to give food to the hungry (social responsibility) has *evangelistic* implications, since good works of love, if done in the name of Christ, are a demonstration and commendation of the Gospel. Thus, evangelism and social responsibility, while distinct from one another, are integrally related in our proclamation of, and obedience to, the Gospel. The partnership is, in reality, a marriage.

Thus, there can be no doubt that since social concern presupposes a Christian social conscience and discipleship and is a consequence and aim of evangelism, evangelism must take logical priority. Also, because social concern relates to the supreme and ultimate need of all humankind for the saving grace of Jesus Christ, acceptance of his grace will determine a person's eternal destiny. We should, however, never have to choose between satisfying physical hunger and spiritual hunger, or between healing bodies and saving souls, since an authentic love for our neighbor will lead us to serve him or her as a whole person. In practice, as in the public ministry of Jesus, evangelism and social engagement are inseparable, and can mutually support and strengthen each other.

A recent study by Miller and Yamamori has furnished unmistakable confirmation of a healthy integration of evangelism and social engagement in the Pentecostal movement. At the conclusion of a four-year, extensive grassroots research journey, covering various expressions of Pentecostalism in twenty different countries in Africa, Asia, Latin America and East Europe, the authors concluded that:

. . . there is an emergent movement within Pentecostal churches worldwide that embraces a holistic understanding of the Christian faith. Unlike the Social Gospel tradition of the mainline churches, this movement seeks a balanced approach to evangelism and social action that is modelled after Jesus' example of not only preaching about the coming kingdom of God but also ministering to the physical needs of the people he encountered.[16]

In the midst of a world with dire needs, Pentecostals are making a difference. They are healing the sick, uplifting the powerless, rescuing children at risk, fighting against AIDS and other deadly diseases, serving the needs of the poorest of the poor. But they are also preaching the good news of Jesus, delivering the demonized, making disciples of Jesus, planting new churches, taking the Gospel to unreached people groups, offering hope to the hopeless.

Since education is for mission it must generate creative and fervent missionary engagement and make a difference in a world full of need! Transforming mission is a passionate commitment to furthering the mission of Christ in our world.

Conclusion: Collaborating with God's World-Changing Project

I believe the onus is on the practitioners—church leaders, lay people and grass-root level workers to initiate a radical movement

---

[16]Donald E. Miller and Tetsunao Yamamori, *Global Pentecostalism: The New Face of Christian Social Engagement* (Berkeley: University of California Press, 2007), 212.

for change in TE systems which fail to deliver. If you do not like the product of TE institutions and systems tell theological educators what you think needs to be changed. If they don't listen, then TE institutions and systems run the risk of being simply ignored! What I am suggesting is not as radical as it may appear at first. It is, in fact, already happening. Let those of us involved in TE read the writing on the wall—change or perish!

TE was intended to be a transforming experience—one that transforms our lives and ultimately our world permanently. TE only has legitimacy to the extent that it effectively furthers the kingdom mission of God in our world.

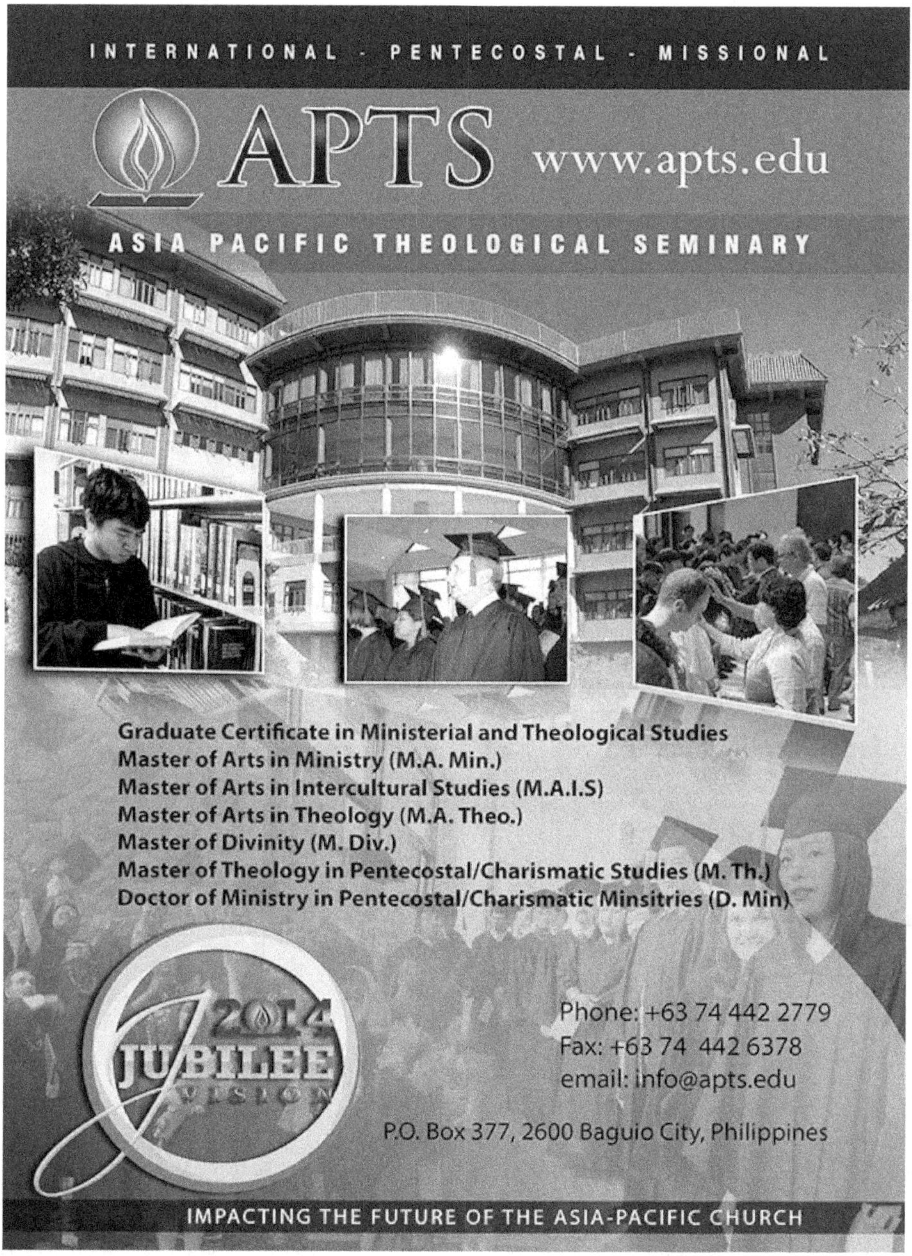
INTERNATIONAL - PENTECOSTAL - MISSIONAL
APTS
www.apts.edu
ASIA PACIFIC THEOLOGICAL SEMINARY
Graduate Certificate in Ministerial and Theological Studies
Master of Arts in Ministry (M.A. Min.)
Master of Arts in Intercultural Studies (M.A.I.S)
Master of Arts in Theology (M.A. Theo.)
Master of Divinity (M. Div.)
Master of Theology in Pentecostal/Charismatic Studies (M. Th.)
Doctor of Ministry in Pentecostal/Charismatic Minsitries (D. Min)
2014
JUBILEE
VISION
Phone: +63 74 442 2779
Fax: +63 74 442 6378
email: info@apts.edu
P.O. Box 377, 2600 Baguio City, Philippines
IMPACTING THE FUTURE OF THE ASIA-PACIFIC CHURCH

APTS Press Monograph Series Book 3
New from APTS Press

UNDERSTANDING THE IGLESIA NI CRISTO
What They Really Believe and How They Can Be Reached

ANNE C. HARPER

A Theology of the Spirit in Doctrine and Demonstration
Essays in Honor of Wonsuk and Julie Ma

Edited by **Teresa Chai**

APTS Press Monograph Series Book 1

Theology in Context

In this book, Dave Johnson discusses a biblical response to Folk Catholicism in the Philippines. Specific topics include what the Bible says about:
- All Saint's Day and the dead returning to their gravesites
- How Filipinos have been transformed by the power of God within their own cultural setting
- Praying to Mary and the saints
- Demon Possession
- Town Fiestas
- Sickness and Healing
- And much more!

About the Author

Dave Johnson, D-Miss, has been an Assemblies of God (USA) missionary to the Philippines since 1994 and has conducted extensive research on lowland Filipino culture. He is also the author of Led by the Spirit: The History of the American Assemblies of God Missionaries in the Philippines and is the managing editor of the Asian Journal of Pentecostal Studies, the theological journal of the Asia Pacific Theological Seminary in Baguio City, Philippines. He can be contacted at www.apts.edu or through his own website, www.daveanddebbiejohnson.com.

Theology in Context: A CASE STUDY in the PHILIPPINES

Now available at:

ICI Ministries
2909 Raffles Corp. Center
Emerald Ave., Ortigas Center
Pasig City
Tel. (632) 914 9800

ICI Distribution Center, Valenzuela
BBC Compound, Gov. I Santiago St.
Malinta, Valenzuela City
Tel. (632) 292-8509/
294-6137/444-9139

APTS Bookstore
444 Ambuklao Road
Baguio City

For other locations please contact us at www.apts.edu.

APTS Press Monograph Series Book 2

LEAVE A LEGACY
Increasing Missionary Longevity

Russ Turney

In this second volume of the new APTS Press Monograph Series, Dr. Russ Turney presents a compelling case study of why some missionaries leave the field far too soon. Normal attrition occurs because of health problems, retirement, or the obvious call of God to go elsewhere. However, Turney notes that far too often missionaries leave due to interpersonal conflicts with their colleagues or nationals, problems with authority and other issues that, Turney contends, could be significantly reduced. He then presents an excellent strategy for dealing with these and other issues, enabling missionaries to continue in their calling long term and finish well.

This strategy will help equip not only missionaries and mission leaders from both the West and the Majority World, but also pastors and church members who love and support missionaries and who want to learn how to strengthen them better through prayer and action. Anyone who shares the warm hearted conviction that missionaries can and should leave a legacy will benefit from this book.

Now available at:

APTS BOOKSTORE
444 Ambuklao Road Baguio City

Jet Bookstore
Porto Vaga, Session Road
Baguio City

ICI Bookstore
BBC Compound,
Malinta, Valenzuela City

CPSIA information can be obtained
at www.ICGtesting.com
Printed in the USA
LVHW101031301219
642025LV00021BA/1273/P

9 781532 633959